**Stripe
Press**

Ideas for progress
San Francisco, California
press.stripe.com

Get Together

—
How to build a community
with **your people.**

Bailey Richardson
Kevin Huynh
Kai Elmer Sotto

Summary

Although communities feel magical, they don't come together by magic. *Get Together* is a guide to cultivating a community—people who come together over what they care about. Whether you're starting a run crew, helping online streamers connect with fans, or sparking a movement of K-12 teachers, the secret to getting people together is this: build your community *with* people, not for them. In *Get Together*, the People & Company team provides stories, prompts, and principles for each stage of cultivating a passionate group of people. Every organization holds the potential to build and sustain a thriving community. *Get Together* shows readers how companies and customers, artists and fans, or organizers and advocates can join forces to accomplish more together than they could have alone.

About the Authors

Bailey Richardson, Kevin Huynh, and Kai Elmer Sotto comprise People & Company, an agency that helps organizations build communities. They've helped create and support communities of investors, entrepreneurs, teachers, caregivers, dog walkers, runners, surfers, and more. Bailey brings her expertise as a storyteller and researcher. She helped shape the communities around Instagram, IDEO, and Pop-Up Magazine. Kevin breathes strategy and structure. He advises groups that build empowered communities, and in the past he operationalized CreativeMornings, rolling out events in 100 cities. Kai focuses on how true communities fuel growth for companies. He helped pioneer Facebook's growth discipline and launch Instagram's business internationally.

Courage

"One of the greatest gifts anybody can give is the inspiration to develop courage. If people feel comfortable enough to develop some courage, then they can do anything they really want to do—why, they can devise their own lives."

—Maya Angelou
  Author, poet, and activist

For our families, who developed our courage: Lainey, Bruce, Perry, Sheila, Chris, Jeff, Yoko, Robert, Diana, Laarnie, Bella, and Kaila.

—Bailey, Kevin, and Kai

Get Together
How to build a community *with* your people
© 2019 People & Company

First published in 2019 in hardcover
in the United States of America
by Stripe Press/Stripe Matter Inc.

Stripe Press
Ideas for progress
San Francisco, California
press.stripe.com

Printed in Canada
ISBN: 978-1-7322651-9-6

First Edition

Preface

Why build a community?

Over the last few years, the three of us have spent a lot of time with people who get people together. There was the night we performed a rendition of John Lennon and Yoko Ono's "Imagine" alongside hundreds of amateur singers at a rec center in the Toronto suburbs. Or the afternoon we spent with the journalist Lola Omolola at her home in Chicago, where she moderates a private Facebook group comprising 1.8 million Nigerian women. Or the winter evening we spent running down Manhattan's 190th Street with a neighborhood run crew.

We sought out these extraordinary people to sharpen our understanding of how to build thriving communities like theirs. Today, the meaning of "community" can be ambiguous. But true communities are simply groups of people who keep coming together over what they care about. The most vibrant communities offer members a chance to act on their passions with one another.

Our conversations with these different clubs, networks, and societies have led to one big takeaway. The secret to getting people together is this: build your community *with* people, not *for* them.

Amateurs try to manage a community, but great leaders create more leaders. Nearly every challenge of building a community can be met by asking yourself, "How do I achieve this by working *with* my people, not doing it *for* them?" In other words, approach community-building as progressive acts of collaboration—doing more *with* others every step of the way.

The implication is simple yet significant. Harvard professor Robert D. Putnam describes the value of reciprocal relationships with the term "social capital." He compares social capital to other well-known forms of capital: "Just as a screwdriver (physical capital) or a college education (human capital) can increase productivity (both individual and collective), so too social contacts affect the productivity of individuals and groups."[1] Like other forms of capital, social capital is an asset. Alone, we are limited. With others, we extend our capacity. Certainly, you can accomplish great things without a thriving community alongside you. But if you join forces—as company and customers, artist and fans, organizer and advocates—you'll do more together than you ever could alone. Plus, you'll likely have more fun in the process.

The throughline of our book is this simple concept: "build with." It lives in each of the recommendations we make as we take you through three stages of building a community: sparking the flame, stoking the fire, and passing the torch.

The insights we offer are a distillation of what we've learned from participating in, coaching, and researching hundreds of communities. In our early days, we grew the global communities around Instagram, CreativeMornings, and eBay. In our work together since teaming up as People & Company, we've helped clients big and small—from companies like Nike to nonprofits like Edcamp—start and scale their communities.

You'll notice that in this book we *do not* dig into why humans need community, analyze the current trend of declining communities, or dissect how organized communities achieve political change. There are wiser experts on those topics. Instead, we want to help you with the practical decisions about what your community needs next.

---

1   *Bowling Alone: The Collapse and Revival of American Community* by Robert D. Putnam.

Community builders go by many names. Whether you see yourself as an aspiring founder, organizer, community manager, host, or people person, in this book we'll refer to you as a leader.

Remember: the community you crave won't form without someone willing to take the first step. And, as is true when you build a fire, there's an order of operations you can follow to cultivate communities that burn bright. We wrote this handbook to guide you on that journey. *You* can spark a community. Don't sit back and wait for one to appear. You're the difference.

Let's get started.

—Bailey, Kevin, and Kai
  People & Company

To dig deeper into any of the communities we mention in this book, visit *gettogetherbook.com*. You can listen to interviews, read full transcripts, and find out how to get involved.

"Fires can't be made with dead embers, nor can enthusiasm be stirred by spiritless men."

—Baldwin

I

Spark the flame

Getting together

To spark a fire, you need to gather kindling. Likewise, to start your community, you need to get your people together. These initial steps are the same whether you're starting a run club or connecting online creators. Pinpoint people you share a purpose with, do something together, and get them talking.

But what if no one shows up? What if other people aren't as passionate as you are? Don't let that fear stop you (or your organization) from trying to get people together. Although communities feel magical, they won't come together by magic. In this early stage, there's no substitute for a courageous leader (like you!) who takes the first step.

Chapter 1

Pinpoint your people

Growing up in New York City's Washington Heights neighborhood, Hector Espinal never imagined that he'd one day become a runner. "I have never been athletic. I've never played any sports. All the men in my family are really into sports but me, so I've always kind of been the black sheep," Hec tells us.[2] He and his friends felt that their neighborhood discouraged a healthy lifestyle, with fast-food joints on every corner and few public spaces to play in.

After Hec went through a tough breakup when he was 23, his sister encouraged him to start running with her to get healthy. Then she went back to school, and Hec was left to run alone. "I knew for a fact that if I ran by myself, I would run a couple of blocks and then start walking, or just turn back," he tells us. So he started asking friends to join him. "I was going on social media and publicly asking people to help me lose weight. I would write in my Notes app, 'Meet me at 168th and Broadway. We're going for a run on the bridge.'" Then Hec would screenshot the note, text it to everyone he knew, and post it on Facebook.

Hec stuck with it week in and week out, and eventually he had a group of regulars joining his runs. The composition of that early run crew made for a remarkable sight. The members were people of all experience

---

2   Hector Espinal on the *Get Together* podcast, episode 6.

"When WRU Crew started, it was about me getting fit," Hector says. "But over the last five years, I've been able to see more of the world and to help my community more than I ever thought I would have been able to."

Photos by Kai Elmer Sotto

levels, ages, and ethnicities, who, like Hec, were truly excited to be running with others in their neighborhood. As Hec explains:

> Running uptown isn't normal, especially our kind of social running. You might see one middle-aged white person running along Riverside Drive on a long run, but you never saw anyone running on Broadway, Amsterdam, or Fort Washington Avenue. So when people started seeing a big group of us running, it was very, very different from what they were used to.

By serving an unmet need in their neighborhood, Hec and his friends were the kindling for something that would grow to be much bigger.

We Run Uptown, or WRU Crew, the run club that Hec sparked six years ago with those early runners, meets every week, even through the dead of winter. As many as 200 runners gather at the same spot on Mondays at 7:15 p.m. The diverse group runs the streets, to the sound of supportive hoots and hollers from folks in the neighborhood.

If you want to spark your own community, you'll need to first pinpoint your people. Find your kindling—those early allies who care about what you care about enough to manifest your idea for a community into an actual gathering of human beings. Though there may not be many of them, the first people you involve are consequential. They will set the tone and direction for the future of your group.

To figure out who to focus on, start with two questions:

1. *Who* do I want to get together?

2. *Why* are we coming together?

For Hector, the answers were straightforward: he brought together neighbors and friends who also craved motivation to start running. Your answers will be different. No matter your community-building endeavor, the original leader should start with a clear *who*, then craft a *why* with that *who* in mind.

Order of operations

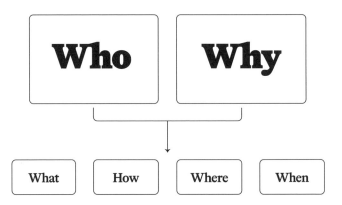

Identifying your *who*

Building a community isn't about you and what you can do; rather, it's dependent upon what you *and* your people can do. So let's get specific about who those people are, before jumping into what you'll do together.

At this stage, you are looking for a team of passionate allies who will show up for this community even before it has gained momentum.

You can find your team of allies by asking yourself a series of more targeted questions:

1. *Who* do I care about?

2. *Who* do I share an interest, identity, or place with?

3. *Who* do I want to help?

Whether you decide on your *who* through personal reflection, dialogue, business strategy, or even data analysis, one lesson remains the same: don't try to fake the feeling. Genuine passion attracts passionate people. If you rally your community because you have a damn good reason to, sincerity will permeate your efforts.

It may take time to find your *who*

If your established organization is interested in fostering a community, how do you pinpoint the right group of people to start with from a sea of existing customers, users, or volunteers?

It took four years of twists and turns for the founders of Justin.tv to realize that the kindling for a community was right in front of them. Launched in 2007, Justin.tv started as a 24/7 show of co-founder Justin Kan's life. Soon, Justin and his fellow creators opened the platform up so that other people could do what he had been doing—stream their lives from webcams, mobile phones, and TVs to the internet for others around the world to watch.

Justin.tv's data revealed that the platform's early users loved to watch one another stream live games, from professional sports like soccer, basketball, and football to, surprisingly, video games. "People hooked up their Xboxes and started broadcasting. We had never even thought of that," Justin.tv co-founder Emmett Shear later told *Forbes*.[3] Video game streamers brought energy to the platform. They were the allies who the Justin.tv team would invest in and build a community with. By 2011, the video gaming category had grown so quickly that Justin.tv's founders decided to launch a new gaming-focused platform called Twitch, which Emmett is now the CEO of.

Now, 12 years after the launch of Justin.tv, nearly 500,000 streamers go live *every day* on Twitch.[4] These streamers play games like *StarCraft II* and *Street Fighter* while their own communities of viewers follow along live. In addition to tuning in, viewers chat with one another and interact with the streamers. More than a million people—streamers and viewers—are on the Twitch site at any given moment, spending time together. They also meet up in person at esports arenas and the company's annual TwitchCon events across the globe.

---

3   "The ESPN of Video Games" by David M. Ewalt, *Forbes*.
4   "The Twitch Holiday Spectacular," Twitch, twitch.tv.

Twitch has invested in a community of streamers, like Mike (@Veritas), a robotics engineer and Twitch Partner. "I hated feeling like I was a hermit at home playing alone. As soon as multiplayer came out and I was able to boot up a game with friends, gaming became a social activity," he says.

Photo courtesy of Veritas

Twitch has even accepted an elite group of streamers into the Twitch Partner Program. Among other benefits, Partners are able to unlock additional ways to earn revenue, a portion of which goes to Twitch.[5] If these Partners succeed in growing their viewers and revenue, so will Twitch.

Justin.tv doubled down on cultivating a community of gamers when the founders examined *who* was most engaged and then aligned the mission of their business with that group's motivations.

Whether you work at a platform company like Twitch or at a small business or nonprofit, you may feel surrounded by potential *whos*. Each pocket of people could flourish into a community. So, who do you start with?

---

5   "Joining the Affiliate Program," Twitch, help.twitch.tv.

Focus on two criteria:

1. **Who brings the energy—who are the people who already engage, contribute, or attend?**
    Don't try to conjure motivation out of thin air. Start with keen participants.

2. **Assuming that the community flourishes, who will you stick with?**
    Cultivating a community is a long-term play. Who does your organization's future rely on (e.g., power users, loyal customers, key donors, passionate employees)? Who do you want to invest in?

Only start this work when you and your organization are eager to collaborate with a specific group of people for the long haul. Like most relationships, communities don't form overnight; they take time to flourish. You'll need to stay invested in these people if you want to bring a community to life.

When you know *who* your community brings together, it's time to pin down exactly *why* you're teaming up.

Defining your *why*

Thriving communities demand a shared purpose, an answer to the question "Why are we coming together?"

"Shared" is the key word. Your purpose needs to be something that your people will want to work on *with* you, not a selfish or one-sided idea hatched by a single leader. If the purpose only serves you, your community-building efforts will fall flat. But the more this purpose resonates with your *who*, the more likely you are to spark a community.

This purpose may be social accountability. Today, WRU Crew exists so that its runners can motivate each other to stay healthy while building stronger ties in a changing neighborhood.

Perhaps the purpose is about creating value. Twitch collaborates with its top streamers to create and promote great content. Revenue generated from that content sustains the business and supports its gamers.

Alternatively, the purpose might center on effecting change. One of our favorite activist communities is the Surfrider Foundation. In 1984, three surfers started Surfrider to stop development and pollution at their home break in Malibu, California.[6] Today, there are 190 Surfrider chapters and clubs, with 500,000 activists and supporters advocating for positive environmental change. Chapters share resources and insights, and form coalitions to push forward the same purpose: protect the world's oceans, waves, and beaches.[7]

In order to make sure that your community's purpose is grounded in your people's needs, and that it expresses what you can accomplish together, consider:

1. **What do my people need more of?**

2. **What's the change we desire?**

3. **What's the problem only we can solve together?**

When you have a strong hunch about *who* you want to get together and *why* you are gathering, you are better equipped to decide *what* to do next.

Make your list of names

Don't underestimate the power of personal outreach when you're trying to spark a community. You truly become a community leader only when you establish your first early ally.

---

6   Chad Nelsen on the *Get Together* podcast, episode 7.
7   "Mission," Surfrider Foundation, surfrider.org.

Write down your community's purpose

"Our community brings together

Who   _____

_____

_____

so that we can

Why   _____

_____

_____ ."

Example: "Our community brings together
fans of the Mola mola fish
so we can
celebrate its magnificence every day."

So who's on your shortlist for this community? What are the names of those early allies—your community's kindling? Who comes to mind first when you think of the people you want to invite to do something with you?

No matter if you're working solo or backed by an organization, your first members will probably stem from existing relationships, the people you already know. That personal connection eases people into taking the leap to participate in something new. Your list might start with close friends who share your passion, or with some of the most engaged users of your app. Make it real: jot down their names and contact information.

That said, you can't predict every person in your network who will feel a pull toward your community's purpose. So go wider and send out a signal. This can take the form of a blog or social media post, an email to that starter list of allies, or a physical sign. Share your hunch about *who* you want to get together and *why*. If they or someone they know wants an invite to that first activity, let them sign up or get in touch. The people who care are more powerful than the people who don't. They alone will help you build a community from scratch.

Balancing inclusion and exclusion

Because many communities start with friends and existing connections, it's possible that your group will feel homogenous in its early days. If that's the case, how do you diversify? In his book *Bowling Alone*, Robert D. Putnam references a bridging and bonding framework, which he attributes to Ross Gittell and Avis Vidal, for understanding what makes communities more diverse.

As Putnam describes, communities dedicated to *bridging* bring different kinds of people together so that they can share assets, ideas, skills, and information. Putnam cites choirs and service groups as examples of bridging communities. These groups tend to attract diverse members and be "outward looking" in their approach.

32

On the other hand, communities focused on *bonding* connect similar types of people for solidarity, reciprocity, and social support. These communities are typically "inward looking and tend to reinforce exclusive identities and homogeneous groups." We've interviewed or coached many communities primarily oriented around bonding, from a meetup for women in tech to a queer dinner club.

Putnam points out that, in practice, communities bond and bridge across different dimensions. They are not "either-or" categories. Internet chat groups, for example, "may bridge across geography, gender, age, and religion," but also bond through being "homogeneous in education and ideology."

Bonding is powerful because it's a kind of "superglue," offering strength and support to people experiencing pain, loneliness, or vulnerability. But Putnam warns that groups focused on extreme bonding run the risk of creating "strong out-group antagonism"—that is, animosity toward outsiders. For example, the Ku Klux Klan is cited as a bonding community. These malevolent, hostile communities attract members who not only bond over a stringent definition of who they are but also codify a purpose to hate, harm, or exclude who they are not. Not cool.

If you believe in promoting diversity and inclusivity (like we do), how do you define a safe space for certain people while stewarding your new community away from an exclusionary identity?

Continually revisit these questions:

1. **What dimensions are my community members bonding over unintentionally?**
   Be conscious of how your community lacks diversity, and probe all possible causes. For example, you may have intended to create a community for online knowledge sharing, but find that your volunteer editors skew overwhelmingly male, diminishing the breadth and integrity of the information on your site.

2. **How can I challenge my community to diversify?**
    The very first members you attract may feel homogenous, but you don't have to keep it that way. Seek opportunities to bridge, whether it be across genders, cultures, professional backgrounds, ages, or socioeconomic situations. Collaborate with existing members to proactively invite and welcome new types of people who connect with your purpose. (See **Chapter 4: Attract new folks** for more on how to take these steps.)

WRU Crew may have started with Hec's social circle uptown, but it has since expanded to include hundreds of people from different neighborhoods, classes, races, and age groups.

That decision to be welcoming wasn't an obvious or spontaneous one. Hec and his co-founder, Josh Mock, actively decided that WRU Crew should reflect their own neighborhood but also welcome new members of all kinds. They make that commitment to diversity explicit in the photos they post and with their public messaging: "All paces are welcome, join and bring a friend."[8] This dedication has trickled down and permeated the group's culture. Every time we've taken the train up to Bodega Pizza for one of the group's Monday runs, various WRU Crew runners make a point to greet us, introduce themselves, and ensure that we feel welcome. As Hec explains:

> I've had a drug dealer sit down with a surgeon for pizza and beer after our runs. They don't even know what each other does for a living because that wasn't what they wanted to talk about. Me and Josh just laugh because these are two people who would never otherwise be talking to each other. But that's what the running community does. It brings people from all walks of life, from all ages, together.

---

8   "Monday Series," We Run Uptown, werunuptown.com.

Without leaders like Hec who take pride in the diversity and evolution of their members, groups risk maintaining the same composition that they started with. You will need to set the tone with your early group if you want to attract and welcome new types of people. Keep that responsibility at the forefront as you rally, nurture, and evolve your community.

Review Pinpoint your people

If you're going to build a community with a group of people, you'll need to know who they are and identify a purpose that will bring them together.

Before getting caught up in what you'll do together, try to answer the following questions:

1. *Who* **do you want to get together?**
   As an individual . . .

   > Who do I care most deeply about?

   > Who do I share an interest, identity, or place with?

   > Who do I want to help?

   Or as an organization . . .

   > Who brings the energy—who are the people who already engage, contribute, or attend?

   > Assuming the community flourishes, who will we stick with?

2. *Why* **are you all coming together?**
   WRU Crew gathers runners to motivate each other. Twitch rallies video gamers so they don't have to game alone. Identify the shared purpose that your people will work together to realize.

   > What do my people need more of?

   > What's the change we desire?

   > What's the problem only we can solve together?

Notes

_____

_____

_____

_____

_____

_____

_____

_____

_____

_____

_____

_____

_____

_____

_____

_____

_____

_____

Chapter 2

Do something together

By now, you know *who* comprises your community and *why* you're teaming up. You've gathered your kindling. It's time to spark a fire by rallying people to do something together—online or IRL—for the first time.

Communities form around shared activities. Sometimes the activity is impossible to do alone. Other times the activity is fine solo but 10 times better when done with others.

Hec makes the grueling, solitary act of running easier (and more fun) with WRU Crew. Twitch enables isolated video gamers to interact while they play. Later in this book, you'll meet communities that share in other activities: testing recipes, creating magazines, navigating personal finances, even admiring clouds. Members realize their community's purpose through the thing that they do *together*. In other words, kindred spirits operating in silos aren't a community (yet).

To determine the central shared activity for your community, ask yourself: What is something your people crave that would be better performed or experienced as a group?

Jean is pictured at a meeting in Louisville, Kentucky, in 1969.

Photo by Phillip Harrington/Alamy Stock Photo

The meeting that kick-started thousands more

We're not fans of people feeling pressure to diet, but the reach of the Weight Watchers (now called WW) community is undeniably impressive. A WW team member tells us that 30,000 in-person workshops take place every week around the world. These meeting spots are everywhere, from big cities (London, England) to remote towns (Sulphur, Oklahoma).

How did WW get its start? The modern, massive community can be traced back to one small meeting held in the founder's Queens, New York, apartment in 1961.

Jean Nidetch was finally able to lose the weight she'd been hoping to for years when, in her late 30s, she checked into a city-run obesity clinic. Excited by her own success, she decided to share the diet program with six friends who were also struggling with weight loss. "I picked my friends carefully... because I was afraid no one would come," Nidetch writes in her autobiography.[9] "They all came."

That night in her living room, Jean created a supportive environment that encouraged these women to be honest and vulnerable about their difficulties with weight management. "Each of them had a story to tell about eating that they had been too ashamed to tell anyone else before," Jean would later write. "It was just such a great relief for us to be able to confess these things for the first time and get over the embarrassment." Jean felt for the other members of the group, who, like her, had for years been left to worry and wonder privately about what they could do to lose weight. This safe space to openly talk to and support one another was "uncharted territory" in the early 1960s, and was the spark for the international WW community that we know today.

Jean's initial group pledged to gather weekly to talk about their successes and disappointments while trying her weight loss plan. Within two months, up to 40 women were traveling to Jean's apartment to meet multiple times a week. She also began to get calls from people around New York City who had heard of her meetings and wanted to learn more. On a May morning in 1963, in a rented space above a movie theater in Little Neck, Queens, Jean hosted the first WW meeting that was open to the public. More than 400 people lined up outside the building. To cover costs, Jean charged a $2 admission fee.

Soon, graduates of the program were asking to take the WW format to new towns. By 1967, just six years after that first meeting in Jean's apartment, WW was in 35 countries. One year later, the company went public.

Today, social support remains at the center of WW meetings around the world. As our friend Amy Reeder, a comics artist and WW member, tells us, "A big part of meetings is just members speaking up and giving advice when others have questions or low times." In facilitating these

---

9   *The Jean Nidetch Story: An Autobiography* by Jean Nidetch.

supportive interactions, WW perpetuates the spirit of openness and sharing that made Jean's first meeting so special.

Design your first activity

Whether you decide to host the inaugural run for your club or launch a website for fellow superfans, the first thing you do to rally the group largely depends on the purpose of your community.

But there are three principles that any first community activity should integrate in order to start your group on a collaborative path:

1. **Make it** *purposeful.*
   Tie the activity back to *why* your community teamed up in the first place. What goal or outcome becomes possible only when this specific group of people gets together? Make this purpose clear to participants so that they can own it, too.

2. **Make it** *participatory.*
   Don't just talk *at* people. You gathered them because they're passionate, just like you! Give them the chance to contribute to the purpose you share.

3. **Make it** *repeatable.*
   One-offs are the enemy. Relationships need time to flourish, and it'll take a few cycles for some folks to warm up and begin actively contributing. Design the first activity with the intent to repeat it with your people over and over.

Make your purpose loud and clear

In 2004, Gavin Pretor-Pinney, a designer and writer with a love for clouds, was encouraged by a friend to speak about his obsession at a literary festival in Cornwall. In hopes of drawing a crowd, Gavin dreamt up an enticing title for his talk: "The Inaugural Lecture of the Cloud Appreciation Society." Why celebrate clouds? "I always felt that clouds are a beautiful part of nature that we can become blind to," Gavin tells us.[10]

The title worked. Gavin's talk was chock-full of attendees. After entertaining the crowd with his passion for clouds, Gavin invited audience members to claim an official society pin. He was bombarded. People asked him for more information about his Cloud Appreciation Society, and Gavin had to tell them that the society didn't exist . . . yet.

Gavin went home and immediately set up a simple website. To encourage cloud-lovers to share their love for clouds, he included a gallery where people could submit their own photographs of the sky. In addition, Gavin made sure that the site put the group's purpose front and center. The society's manifesto reads, "We believe that clouds are unjustly maligned and that life would be immeasurably poorer without them."[11] Gavin explains, "The fact that we appreciate an underappreciated part of nature gives the society a reason to exist."

Visitors to the site who connected with this purpose could fill out a form and pay a small fee in exchange for a welcome package (complete with a society pin) and official membership number. After just a few months, the society grew to 2,000 paying members. Member enthusiasm, playful merchandise, and press coverage helped spread the word. By 2016, membership had reached 40,000.[12]

---

10   Gavin Pretor-Pinney on the *Get Together* podcast, episode 2.

11   "Cloud Appreciation Society Manifesto," Cloud Appreciation Society, cloudappreciationsociety.org.

12   "The Amateur Cloud Society That (Sort Of) Rattled the Scientific Community" by Jon Mooallem, *The New York Times Magazine*.

"People feel their membership reflects well on them because it shows they look at the world in a slightly different way from others," Gavin Pretor-Pinney says. "It shows that they're sensitive to the natural world. It shows that they've got imagination, because they can see this aspect of nature has a magical quality to it."

Photo courtesy of Gavin Pretor-Pinney

44

With your first activity, you have an opportunity to make a statement about why your community comes together. Gavin drew focus to the Cloud Appreciation Society's purpose when he launched the group, and then he wove that purpose through each of his community's first activities. By making the society's purpose clear and accessible, Gavin made it easy for potential members to find the society and understand whether they'd want to join.

Follow Gavin's lead. Don't be shy about telegraphing your community's purpose and choosing a first activity that relates back to it.

Encourage people to participate from the start

Growing up, Ryan Fitzgibbon could never find stories about "what it's actually like to be gay—to get broken up with, to go on a first date, to come out."[13] Ryan didn't see himself anywhere in the media landscape, and he wanted to change that.

In 2012, he announced *Hello Mr.*, a magazine "about men who date men." As Ryan puts it, he set out to "rebrand" the gay community with new stories and new aesthetics. "It was a statement for me to not have rainbows anywhere in the magazine in the first issue," Ryan explains.

After establishing the magazine's name, mission statement, and visual characteristics, Ryan started telling friends about his idea. "It just became so clear that people felt the need for this. It was almost like I didn't have to explain, because they understood immediately," he says. "That made it apparent that I needed to hurry up and make *Hello Mr.* happen."

At this point, Ryan could have run full steam ahead and produced the magazine on his own. But instead of making something *for* the future readers of *Hello Mr.*, he decided to team up *with* them to make *Hello Mr.* a reality.

"When *Hello Mr.* hit the shelf at the Barnes & Noble in my hometown, my mom went to buy it, and she sent me a photo of it on the front shelf," Ryan tells us. "Every other magazine featured a shirtless man with a chiseled body, and then there was *Hello Mr.* just sitting in the front being all coy and confident, very minimal and approachable. It made me weep."

Photo courtesy of Ryan Fitzgibbon

Ryan worked with contributors to create 30% of the magazine's content, before launching a Kickstarter campaign for funding to finish the rest. Those early contributors, many of whom were also queer, were crucial to spreading the word. "They were accountable for this thing happening and became our greatest ambassadors when it came to promoting [the Kickstarter campaign]," Ryan tells us.

The Kickstarter project made his vision for *Hello Mr.* clear, and issued an open call for submissions. Within days, Ryan was overwhelmed with interest. He received over 100,000 words from hopeful writers before the funding campaign even wrapped up. As he describes it, "people felt

---

13   "How Ryan Fitzgibbon built *Hello Mr.* hand-in-hand with its community"
by Bailey Richardson, Medium: People & Company.

Photo courtesy of Kai Elmer Sotto

like there was a new place for them and they rushed in—like a body of water filling in a crater." With help from a community of early contributors, *Hello Mr.* launched to the world within a few months.

Stop thinking about your community as just an audience. Instead, treat these people as collaborators. Even with your first activity, carve out ways for others to participate. People are showing up to realize a shared purpose, not to watch you realize it for them.

Be prepared to repeat

If you want to sustain a community, not just host an epic one-off experience, you'll need to design a core activity that you and your people can repeat from the get-go.

In 2008, Nobu Adilman, Daveed Goldman, and Amanda Burt got a 13-person choir together to sing at a mutual friend's surprise birthday party. Even with such a small group, they knew that they had something

Nobu Adilman recalls, "We did a tribute for Prince at Massey Hall, which is probably the most important venue that has ever existed in Canada. Two thousand people came out to sing 'When Doves Cry.' We ran the night the way we would run it at a tiny little dive bar, and we were able to maintain the intimacy with that many people. I remember being onstage at this venue that was the venue of my dreams as a kid growing up in Toronto, and just thinking if this isn't success, I don't know what is."

Photo by Kai Elmer Sotto

special. Two years later, Nobu and Daveed were still reflecting on that night—so they posted on Facebook asking if anyone wanted to sing in a choir with them, this time at a Toronto real estate office where a friend worked. "We thought maybe some friends would show up and we'd just have a couple beers," Nobu tells us.[14] He and Daveed prepared some minor arrangements to "Nowhere Man" by the Beatles and "Just a Smile" by the Scottish rock band Pilot.

"It was kind of extraordinary what happened that night. People we didn't even know showed up," remembers Nobu. At the end of the evening, "people were so into what we did, which was very little, that they wanted us to do it again the next day." Choir! Choir! Choir! was born.

---

14   Nobu Adilman on the *Get Together* podcast, episode 9.

Photo by Kai Elmer Sotto

Nobu and Daveed were motivated by such a passionate reaction. "We ended up doing it every Tuesday for the next year," Nobu says. By 2012, they were getting hundreds of people together to sing one iconic pop song each week.

Today, Nobu and Daveed continue to repeat the same format they pioneered at their first gathering. To participate in a Choir! Choir! Choir! event, you just show up, pay five dollars for a lyrics sheet (more if the group is touring), rehearse a three-part harmony, and then perform it with a crowd of strangers. Many of the choir's recordings have gone viral, from Prince and David Bowie tributes to sing-alongs led in person by famous musicians, including David Byrne, Rufus Wainwright, and Patti Smith.[15]

---

15   "Breathing New Life Into Pop Songs with Choir! Choir! Choir!" by John Ortved, *The New Yorker.*

Every thriving community organizes essential, repeating activities for its members. If communities are about people coming together, one of the most important things you can do is create ways for them to keep coming together. Repeating activities set the stage for members to deepen their relationships and for the community to gain momentum.

As you make these early attempts to rally people, do so with purpose, enable participation, and be prepared to repeat the activity again, and soon.

Some shared activities are better than others

If the fire doesn't catch with your first activity, we get it. We've been there. (Ask us about the time we hosted a super user happy hour and only two people showed up!)

Remember: big things often start small. Many widespread, thriving communities started with just a handful of participants. WW's Jean Nidetch had six people at her first meeting. Hec from WRU Crew went for that first run with just a few of his sister's friends. Surfrider started with three surfing buddies. If you want to gain momentum, you'll have to keep at it week after week.

Pay attention to feedback, and try to gauge your people's interest objectively. If no one wants to repeat this activity with you, that's a red flag. It's not a community if participants only show up once. (More on this in **Chapter 6: Pay attention to who keeps showing up**.)

If your early attendees aren't hungry for more, go back to the drawing board. Do you really understand your *who*, and *why* they'd want to come together? Is the design of your activity more interesting, more fun, or more meaningful to experience as a group?

The inescapable truth is that you'll have to exceed expectations with your core activity if you want people to show up and keep showing up. This doesn't mean that you need to invest lots of money in a flashy first experience. Instead, do your best to create an undeniably valuable *shared* experience.

While many choirs get together around the world, the preparation, teaching methods, and energy that Nobu and Daveed bring to Choir! Choir! Choir! enable every attendee (even choral amateurs like us) to contribute their voice to a truly moving performance. If what you do as a group amplifies what members experience alone, you're on your way to sparking a community.

Review Do something together

Communities form around shared activities. As you approach designing your first activity, ask:

1. **What is something your people can't do solo? Or that would be better in a group?**
   The more compelling the shared activity, the more likely you are to spark a community.

2. **Is the activity *purposeful*?**
   Tie the activity back to your community's purpose. And communicate that purpose explicitly, as Gavin Pretor-Pinney did when he formed the Cloud Appreciation Society.

3. **Is the activity *participatory*?**
   Encourage people to participate from the start, as Ryan Fitzgibbon did when he worked with early contributors to launch the fundraiser for *Hello Mr.*

4. **Is the activity *repeatable*?**
   Communities need time to take shape. Design the first activity with the intent to repeat it over and over, as Daveed Goldman and Nobu Adilman have succeeded in doing with their traveling Choir! Choir! Choir! format.

Notes

Chapter 3

Get people talking

People participate in communities for a variety of reasons—to sing, to lose weight, to read stories that speak to them. But regardless of what drives people to show up for the first time, the relationships they form are what will bring them back.

Meaningful human connections are sticky. They make us return to shared endeavors, from Weight Watchers to team sports to church. As Scott Heiferman, co-founder of Meetup, told us during a workshop, "people show up for the meetup but they come back for the people."

Through open and ongoing dialogue, a loose group of people with a shared interest can be transformed into a community, teeming with life. If you do the work to get your people talking, members of your community will be able to swap stories, support each other, and pursue collective goals. The richer the 1:1 connections between members, the stronger the community.

To enable all the ways your people can share and collaborate with one another, you'll have to create spaces where members can freely connect on their own time.

Even a kitchen appliance community craves connection

Instant Pot has a cult following. The multipurpose pressure cooker Robert Wang built is so remarkable that it has spurred an outpouring of enthusiasm from fans around the world.

That zeal wasn't a surprise to Robert, due to a core insight he had early on. "Cooking is not a solitary practice. It's very much a social practice," he tells us.[16] "You cook for your family, you cook for your friends, you'll throw a party if you make a dish." Because of the social nature of cooking, Robert knew there was a good chance that news about the Instant Pot could spread through word of mouth, thanks to its most passionate customers. He was right.

The conversations that "Potheads" shared with friends in person also spilled over online. The community's main watering hole is a Facebook group. Robert and his team opened the group in 2015, imagining it as a space where customers separated by geography could help each other with Instant Pot questions—both connecting superfans and lightening the burden on the company's customer support team. Today, more than 1.8 million people of all ages, languages, and backgrounds have joined the Facebook group to share recipes and Instant Pot fandom.[17] Some Potheads name their pots, while others knit sweaters for the appliances.

Robert Wang tells us that his team chose to create a Facebook group after deciding against a Facebook page and an email marketing strategy. "The objective was to get old customers and new customers and non-customers all to talk. For those needs, email marketing wouldn't work and a Facebook page wouldn't work, because in those people aren't talking to each other," Robert says.

This was crystal clear to Robert, but, for many community leaders, getting your most passionate people talking to one another isn't an obvious

---

16   Robert Wang on the *Get Together* podcast, episode 15.
17   "Instant Pot Community," Facebook group, facebook.com.

"I don't think there's much secret. Get the product right, treat the customer well, and get them talking. And that's it," Instant Pot founder Robert Wang once explained to *Inc.*[18]

Photo courtesy of Instant Pot

18   "Here's the Smart Secret behind the Most Successful Product on Amazon" by Bill Murphy Jr., *Inc.*

step. For any community to flourish, it's essential that members have a space where they can speak directly to each other, without having to depend on a founder or leader to play intermediary.

Today, Instant Pot continues to grow despite little advertising, in part because of its commitment to facilitating dialogue among Instant Pot fans. Those direct lines of communication enable community members to inspire and support each other, and provide employees at the company with new insights.

Give members the space, prompts, and structure to start talking

Conversations—like those unfolding daily in the Instant Pot Facebook group—don't start without provocation. Leaders need to lay the groundwork for free-flowing communication between members.

To get your community talking, figure out:

1. **Space**

   Where can members find each other to continue their conversations independently?
   Today, there's no shortage of online communication tools that make this easier than ever: messaging platforms, email lists, forums, Facebook groups. Consider the platforms where your people already spend a lot of their time, and determine which space best supports the media (text, visuals, music, links, etc.) that you expect members to share with one another. There can also be benefits to choosing a discrete space, devoid of the distractions some social platforms have.

2. **Prompts**

   How do I give people an excuse to connect for the first time?
   It's scary to talk to strangers. Guide your members into discussions by modeling what good participation looks like. Craft regular prompts and make introductions for newbies.

3. **Structure**

   What structure would make communication in this space more meaningful?

   When implemented with care, ground rules and moderation can facilitate and reward focused, sincere conversations. Structure also supports healthy debate when conflict arises.

Take an active role in prompting discussion

Lola Omolola, who had previously worked as a journalist in her home country of Nigeria, was living in Chicago in 2014 when she heard that Boko Haram had kidnapped hundreds of Nigerian schoolgirls. Lola felt overwhelmed and decided it was time to act. She remembers, "My initial idea was to create a space where I could find women who were like me, who were as worried about the same thing, so we could all come together and form some sort of a resource."[19]

So Lola started a private Facebook group, Female in Nigeria (FIN), to explore struggles and victories with other Nigerian women. She invited friends, who in turn invited their friends, to join the group—women located mostly in Nigeria, but also throughout the diaspora. But how did she get the first conversations started?

Lola searched the internet for "little snippets from women talking openly about issues that I knew Nigerian women didn't speak openly about." She pulled anecdotes from public posts by Nigerian women on Twitter, Facebook, and blogs, and published the quotes on FIN as prompts awaiting commentary. For instance, Lola reposted a story on FIN about a widow who couldn't rent an apartment because she didn't have a man with her when she met the landlord, and another about a woman who went to a barbershop only to be told by the owner that she needed a permission note from her husband if she wanted to get the haircut she'd requested.

---

19   Lola Omolola on the *Get Together* podcast, episode 3.

"With FIN, I found people who also cared about something that mattered to me all of my life—something I had been alone in worrying about. Suddenly there was validation. Other people wanted to talk about issues that we were all raised with a pinch and a shush to shut up about." Lola Omolola, a former journalist, started the Female In Nigeria (FIN) group on Facebook so that women could share their untold stories without shame or fear.

Photo by Kai Elmer Sotto

When she quoted women's stories like these, Lola tells us, "it got really personal really quickly." Members started adding their own experiences in the comments, and, she says, "those responses were so raw. They were more powerful than the original quotes that I had found on the internet." Lola didn't stop there. She pulled new quotes from FIN's member comments to use as the next prompts for the community.

From day one, Lola served as a role model for what participating in a FIN discussion should look like, posting the quotes she had sourced and encouraging new members to share for the first time. When you create a space for community members to interact, don't stand on the sidelines waiting for people to start their own conversations. Take an active role in prompting discussion. Think about the purpose of your community and introduce the topics that are pivotal to hash out in order to achieve that purpose.

Today, FIN (which now stands for "Female IN" to reflect a broader group of women) has 1.7 million members and gets hundreds of post applications every day.[20] The Facebook group is managed by 10 volunteer moderators. Lola hopes to move forward with FIN by providing social and empowerment events as well as physical centers where women can talk about their experiences in a safe space offline.

Introduce structure to keep conversations meaningful

Structure alone won't ignite lively discussions, but it will support meaningful ongoing dialogue once it's begun.

Bogleheads is a community of investing enthusiasts who extol the low-cost, keep-it-simple finance philosophies of the late John C. Bogle, the founder of the Vanguard Group. The nexus of the Boglehead community is bogleheads.org, an online forum that Taylor Larimore, now in his 90s, helped start 20 years ago.[21]

Thousands of Bogleheads have contributed to forum discussions over the years. Today, new members continue to flock to the site not only because of the wealth of its archives but also for the unusually generous culture of the group. Any newbie who posts a thoughtful finance question (e.g., "How should I invest money that I'm saving up for a down payment on a house?") is likely to receive personalized, timely responses from longtime Boglehead contributors.

---

20   "Female IN (FIN) – Public," Facebook community page, facebook.com.
21   "The Bogleheads®," Bogleheads Wiki, bogleheads.org.

We asked the Bogleheads for the secret to keeping their conversations so helpful and educational. One forum contributor broke it down for us:

1. **Strict rules on what you can't discuss here, specifically politics.**

2. **Moderators who enforce the rules.**

3. **Participants who seem to enjoy helping others.**

The Boglehead forum's public rules provide guardrails surrounding what subjects members are meant to discuss in the space and how to discuss them. Of course, not everyone reads the rules. That's why Bogleheads designate volunteer moderators, who ensure that people respect the rules. (See **Chapter 7: Create more leaders** for how to vet and develop your own leaders.) As Taylor explains to us, the Bogleheads moderators prohibit conversations involving "commercialism, profanity, or topics like politics and religion," which invite arguments and take the conversation away from the purpose of the site, advice and discussion about investment.

By appointing moderators and establishing a code of conduct, you're making a safe space for conflict, which is an essential part of any community. Disagreements among community members can be the seeds of important ideas. Squashing all conflicts will stifle creativity and limit your community's potential to collaborate and address challenges together. That said, lacking the structure to deal with conflicts when they do inevitably arise can lead to disrespectful discourse or, worse, a culture that tears down people willing to speak up.

The goal of structure is to focus conversations (including the hard ones!) on the unique ideas that *your* community wants to explore together. To find the right balance, work with your early members on simple ground rules that describe how your community will both address and work through conflicts that occur in your discussion space. Perhaps, like the Bogleheads, your group is focused on a specific interest, in which case it would be helpful to make clear which topics

"What a joy to go somewhere these days and not have everything reduced to politics. Of course that can feel artificial (certainly politics play an important role in finances), but it's such a brilliant policy for giving and getting advice," Bogleheads forum member TSR shares with us.

Taylor Larimore (right), who has been described as the "king of the Bogleheads," started the forum. He is pictured here in 2013, celebrating with Jack Bogle (left) at the Bogleheads 12 Conference, in Philadelphia.

Photo by Greg Jones

are acceptable for conversation. Also, set clear ground rules about the hurtful or inflammatory communication that's unacceptable within your community.

Two decades after the Bogleheads forum's inception, the conversations there remain meaningful because the watering hole isn't a space to discuss every topic under the sun. Through ongoing dialogue and debate, members continue to do what Jack Bogle strove to do when he started Vanguard: help ordinary investors get a fair shake.

Starter questions for your code of conduct

1. **What's our purpose?**
   Remind members *why* your community exists before dictating specific rules.

2. **What is okay?**
   How should members act? Describe the spirit of your community and introduce etiquette that keeps conversations valuable. (Bogleheads: "Discussions are about issues, not people.")[22]

3. **What is not okay?**
   List behaviors that are not allowed (e.g., no insults or hateful language) to help make members feel confident in joining the community and safe in reporting violations.

4. **How do members report violations?**
   Give members a private way (such as an email address) to report violations. Explain who receives that report.

5. **How will you investigate and enforce the rules?**
   Let members know how you'll collect information on the situation and what consequences to expect when the code of conduct is violated (e.g., a private warning, followed by a temporary ban for a certain number of days).[23]

---

22 "Board Rules," Bogleheads Forum, bogleheads.org.
23 Informed by "Your Code of Conduct," Github's Open Source Guides, opensource.guide/code-of-conduct.

Review Get people talking

Personal relationships bond people in communities. To encourage rich 1:1 relationships within your community, create spaces where members can connect to one another on their own time.

1. **In what *space* will your group members continue their conversations?**
    Where do they already spend their time? Which platform best supports the media that members want to share? Find a space for members to gather, like Instant Pot's Facebook group.

2. **How might you *prompt* strangers to speak up?**
    Give people a reason to talk, and make introductions for newbies, as Lola did with the real quotes from real people that she used to spark conversations in FIN.

3. **What *structure* will focus the conversations?**
    Ground rules, norms, and moderators, like those the Bogleheads forum embraces, can facilitate the sincere, challenging conversations your members seek.

Spark the flame: Hear the full stories

Just getting started with your community? Visit **gettogetherbook.com/spark** to hear more from community leaders on what it took to get their people together.

Listen to Hec describe the very first WRU Crew runs, Lola explain exactly how she got FIN's first members talking, and more.

Stoke the fire

Sticking together

To spark your community, you got people together and helped them start talking. Stay with it! The missing ingredient in many would-be communities is dedication. We put on one-off events or annual fundraisers, but we don't give potential community members the chance to keep showing up or to raise their hands to take on responsibilities.

As your community swells beyond its early membership, the challenge will be to make sure your people stick together. If you can consistently attract authentic folks, encourage a shared sense of identity, and keep a finger on the pulse of the community, you'll stoke the flames, transforming your spark into a roaring fire.

Chapter 4

Attract new folks

A sign of a vibrant community is that new members join because they want to. Aspiring leaders frequently forget the importance of this agency. They plop unknowing people on a list and start calling them a community.

Yet new folks need to be genuinely excited about your shared purpose or they'll never stick with the group. That kind of passion cannot be fabricated or forced. You can't push potential members through a marketing funnel, expecting them to do what you want them to do when you want them to do it.

Instead of a push, create a pull. Don't broadcast a mass message to a faceless audience. Rather, work with your members to collectively send a clear, authentic signal about what your community is all about.

Establish your origin story

Step one in attracting new members is crafting your origin story. Your origin story will give both existing and prospective members the language they need to explain what your community is and why it formed in the first place.

Whether you're sharing your origin story in conversation or publishing it on your website, what's most important is that the story isn't just about you. Marshall Ganz is a Harvard senior lecturer who organized the United Farm Workers alongside Cesar Chavez from 1965 to 1981, and designed the grassroots organizing model for Barack Obama's 2008 presidential campaign. Ganz's current course is titled Organizing: People, Power, Change. In it, he teaches a framework called Public Narrative, which helps students tell stories that will motivate others to join a cause.

"A story of self communicates the values that are calling you to act," he writes in the course notes. "A story of us communicates values shared by those whom you hope to motivate to act. And a story of now communicates the urgent challenge to those values that demands action now."[24]

Ganz believes public narratives communicate three key concepts. When you refine your origin story, follow Ganz's lead:

1. **Tell the story of self.**

   Make it personal. Describe the moment that you started on the path to rally your community. What made you start caring? Bring it to life with personal details.

2. **Tell the story of us.**

   Show that it's bigger than you. What do you believe is made possible when this group comes together? This is also your community's purpose.

3. **Tell the story of now.**

   What's one small, immediate way someone can get involved (e.g., attend a meetup, sign up for a newsletter, sign a petition)? Why should they do so now? This urgency will make people feel the pull to get started right away.

---

24 "Organizing Notes, Spring 2016" handout by Marshall Ganz, Organizing: People, Power, Change.

Serve up your origin story

Once you're satisfied with your narrative, the next step is to make that origin story available to anyone curious about what you stand for.

Share your origin story in one-on-one conversations with strangers, newcomers, and other potential community members. If you gather in person, don't be timid. Grab the mic! At the beginning of the Choir! Choir! Choir! event that we attended in Toronto, Nobu took the time to share with the audience how he and Daveed had come to start their group sing-alongs. Nobu talked about their first event, how they'd evolved since the early days, and why he believes that we need generous, positive gatherings now more than ever.

In that quick, engaging introduction, Nobu covered his stories of self, us, and now for a captive audience. If he hadn't carved out that time, none of us would have understood the depth of what we were a part of that night. But because Nobu made sure to share his origin story, we left the concert inspired *and* equipped to invite our friends and family to the next Choir! Choir! Choir! event.

In most cases, you should also create an online version of your origin story. To begin, research where and how current members discovered your community. Asking members "How did you hear about us?" is a great way to start. Digital analytics can help point you to relevant spaces, too.

Then design a way to share your origin story so that it'll resonate in those places and formats. If people are finding you through a search engine, write a blog post or add your origin story to the "About Us" section of your website. Or turn your origin story into an engaging video that visitors to your social media can watch. These online versions of your story are powerful evergreen artifacts that provide interested people with a clear, quick, easily digestible understanding of who you are whenever they seek it out.

Regardless of whether your origin story is shared online or off, it is your responsibility to make sure it's available *somewhere*. When consistently communicated in this way—connecting self, us, and now—your origin story provides others with the language that they'll need to help spread the word about what makes your community worth joining.

Share the recruiting responsibility

Now that you have your origin story pinned down, here's the secret to spreading the word: attracting others can't just be your job. Ask any traditional marketer, and they'll tell you that word-of-mouth advertising is their most powerful tool. If members are helping you grow your community, you'll reach more people than you ever could alone.

You can't expect people to recruit others without a nudge. Make it clear to members that their active involvement is crucial to ensuring the vitality and success of your community. At your gatherings, online or off, carve out time to make sure existing members know that the more people who attend, the more enjoyable and impactful the experience will be for everyone involved. If your members agree, they'll take that sense of responsibility to heart.

Once members know that they play a role in attracting new folks, your next step is to make sharing easy, even exciting, for them. Serve up the rad photos, videos, or language they'll be excited to use when they tell friends about the community they're a part of.

Aria McManus, an artist and creative director, started Downtown Girls Basketball in 2013. From the beginning, it was a team for women and people who don't identify as male, and "who are specifically bad at basketball," Aria tells us.[25] At the first practice, 30 of Aria's artist and designer friends rolled out to play together. They had so much fun that Aria hosted another game the following week.

---

25   Aria McManus on the *Get Together* podcast, episode 11.

"The team pic was inspired by the old commemorative photos of teams and coaches dressed up in uniform," explains Aria McManus (center with ball), founder of the Downtown Girls Basketball squad.

Photo by Lauren Gesswein

In the five years since, that core group has ballooned to a rotating crew of more than 400 women. Similar teams have popped up in cities like Los Angeles, San Francisco, and London. How?

Each week, without fail, Aria takes a team photo at halftime (so that even players who have to leave early don't get left out). "People always say, 'I haven't come before, I'm not going to be in the team photo,'" Aria explains. "So that photo is a moment to be like, 'No, you're on the team and we're showing that to the world.'" Before practice wraps, she offers to share the team pic with anyone who wants it. Nearly everyone raises their hand. Within an hour of receiving the squad pic, many of the players have posted it on their personal Instagram accounts, coupled with captions describing their experiences.

"The most surprising thing for me was how many people showed up on day one. And that continues to be the most surprising thing—that people are still showing up on day 300. Every time a stranger comes, I'm just like, 'Where did you come from?' It is amazing, and it's a huge motivator to keep me going," says Aria McManus.

Photo by Kai Elmer Sotto

Ask a new player how they found out about the games, and their answer is almost always the same: team pics posted on Instagram. "At first, everyone would just post the photos to say, 'I'm a part of this team,'" Aria tells us. "And then it became a word-of-mouth thing." Week in and week out, that collective storytelling push adds up—trickling awareness spreads to new, artsy, basketball-loving women who keep the Downtown Girls squad vibrant.

Shareable assets allow Downtown Girls Basketball players to avoid starting from scratch every time they tell a story about the community or explain to a potential new member how to get involved.

You can't force people to spread the word. Instead, ask: How can I make it easier for them to do so on their own terms?

Instagram post by baileyelaine
• Ps 142 Amalia Castro

chrisconnolly Tough as hell
psyoko BAMFs
lauragravley #sporty
underfang I 🖤 Downtown Girls Bball
baileyelaine @underfang I 🖤 u ray
baileyelaine @hassanmirza I know her as of today's Bball game!!
hassanmirza @baileyelaine yey! Tell her I say hi! And hi to you too BE
palamac You gotta add @atmccann to ur roster-she's a 👟 ♀️🏀 😍 😉
baileyelaine @palamac I already was asking her about it! @palamac you have to play if you're in town
ak_therealest nice
gettyshotz Hi, the post is beautiful! 👍
hairdewbev Jaaaaaaaammmmn On It!

170 likes
FEBRUARY 11

Add a comment...

Bailey's Instagram post after her first time at Downtown Girls Basketball.

Photo courtesy of Bailey Richardson

Collect the right shareable stories for *your* community

The stories shared by your members will depend on the activities you do together as a community.

It's your job to figure out how to turn your community's unique activities into natural, simple narratives. Here are some starter ideas:

1. **Your community centers around *in-person experiences*.**
    Package up interesting insider content that encapsulates those experiences. For example:

    Choir! Choir! Choir! participants pass around YouTube videos of sing-alongs.

    Downtown Girls Basketball players post up a commemorative team photo after each practice on their personal Instagram accounts.

2. **Your community centers around *training* or *learning*.**
Encourage members to share their efforts. For example:

> Instant Pot community members post their original recipes online for others to test out.

> Cyclists in the Rapha Cycling Club (a community that you'll learn more about in **Chapter 5: Cultivate your identity**) record their workouts on Strava, a social fitness tracking app.

3. **Your community centers around *contributing and sharing content*.**
Then make the content that they contribute simple to reshare and discover. For example:

> Fans following their favorite streamers on Twitch can create short, shareable video clips of choice moments from any broadcast.

> The Bogleheads' extensive archive of financial advice is easily accessed with a simple Google search.

If none of these sharing strategies jumps out as a natural choice for your community, don't fret. Look to your community members for inspiration. They're already passing around stories. That's guaranteed. Dig into how and what they're sharing. Figure out which tools, information, and resources you could offer to boost their storytelling.

Finally, although sharing stories is a powerful way to attract new folks, don't let it compromise the values that your community espouses. For instance, Changemaker Chats is a community of female professionals who gather in 16 cities (and soon even more!) for unfiltered discussions with female leaders about how they've navigated their careers.[26] Co-founder Briana Ferrigno says, "We don't just want to hear success stories—we want to hear the good, the bad, and the ugly. We want to know how resilience is built."[27]

---

26   "All Events," Changemaker Chats, changemakerchat.com.
27   "Changemaker Chats Founders Jessica Johnston and Briana Ferrigno 'Don't Just Want to Hear Success Stories,'" MM.LaFleur: The—M—Dash, mmlafleur.com.

The most important rule at Changemaker Chats is that conversations are off the record. There's no video, audio, or live-tweeting allowed—and that privacy welcomes raw conversations while protecting potentially vulnerable participants.

The Changemaker Chats team still finds ways to create shareable stories by packaging select quotes in a post-event newsletter. But they honor the purpose of the community before chasing growth at any cost.

Wield your spotlight

With a refined origin story and resources for members to spread the word, the foundation to attract new people to your community is in place. Congrats!

You've acted as a storytelling catalyst, collaborating with members to share what your community is all about. Now your job is to put a spotlight on the inspiring people in your community. In creating exposure for these exceptional folks, you'll bring the community to life for others considering joining. And, as a bonus, you'll celebrate what standout participation looks like, which can motivate existing members to deepen their involvement.

Unlike the finite process of establishing an origin story, highlighting community members and their contributions is an ongoing endeavor.

If you want to show that your community is alive and vibrant, you'll need to maintain a steady pulse in your storytelling. Devote resources and time to regularly seeking out new narratives from members of your community and publishing them widely.

Prior to founding People & Company, Bailey spotlighted thousands of Instagrammers as one of Instagram's first employees. She continues to channel her energy today towards helping nascent community leaders share their stories with the world.

Photo by Kai Elmer Sotto

Building a culture of reciprocity

When I joined Instagram as an employee in the beginning of 2012, I walked into an office of 10 or so people: a handful of engineers, one designer, one business lead, and a small community team.

Our community team acted as the conduit between the people using Instagram and the people making it. We answered emails that confused users sent in, read every tweet to @Instagram, wrote rules about what could and could not appear on the site (and enacted those policies, reviewing countless images), and communicated to Instagrammers whenever the app went down or a new feature was ready for them.

But my favorite task was foraging for exceptional Instagrammers. I'd spend hours combing the site for interesting, creative people around the world—everyone from Gedun Wangchuk (@gdax), a monk in Tibet with a passion for photography, to Drew Kelly (@drewkelly), a Californian who at the time was teaching English in Pyongyang and documenting what he saw there, to Shota Tsukamoto, the owner and photographer behind Darcy (@darcytheflyinghedgehog), a photogenic hedgehog in Tokyo. I had never seen images like these before—first-person photographs, uploaded in real time, from people like me, all around the world. They brought to life the unique value of being a part of the Instagram community. You could peer into lives different from yours as if they were your own.

The joyful day that Bailey finally met Andrew Knapp (@andrewknapp) and his dog, Momo, in real life. Bailey found Andrew's creative #FindMomo series and wrote about him on the Instagram blog. Since then, he's published four Find Momo books!

Photo courtesy of Bailey Richardson

isabelitavirtual ✔ • Follow

isabelitavirtual It was an odd relationship.
#WHPpatterns

View all 35 comments

trynidada 🖤 💚 🖤

manilazposts The
#womanwholovescolors 🖤🤍 🤍 🖤 🖤

shoesinart Love

karenschuang This was the visual goal
@dianascho @n8thankim

alessiaglaviano Great @isabelitavirtual
🖤 🖤 🖤

isabelitavirtual #WHPpatterns

isabelitavirtual @quietpoem
@unskilledworker @teklan @tilly2milly
@trynidada Thanks goddesses.You all
are ✨

joselourenco 👌 👌 👌

2,505 likes

MARCH 19, 2016

Add a comment...

"When I received your email telling me that I was going to be featured, the first thing that came to my mind was: 'I'm not invisible,'" says Isabel Martinez (@isabelitavirtual), one of the Instagrammers Bailey discovered. "Up to that moment, Instagram was an abstraction. It was just a company, real people weren't running it. That email was a bridge between us, and I began to feel responsible—like I was a little, but important, part of the Instagram team. We were in this together."

Photo by Isabel Martinez

When I found amazing Instagrammers, I'd feature them on our Suggested Users List, as well as on our company blog (blog.instagram.com) and our own @Instagram account. Those channels put these exceptional people in front of a combined audience of tens of millions of readers. As we grew, I hired people around the world to write stories about more Instagrammers in more languages, from Russian to Japanese, to make sure that our storytelling evolved alongside our community.

Why did we carry out this storytelling? People can't be what they can't see. We wanted to show, not tell, what Instagram was all about. In doing so, we not only offered existing users inspiration, we also signaled to the rest of the world that Instagram was the place to find a window into the world.

We didn't push people to join us. Instead, we consistently made clear what Instagram was about so that people could choose to be a part of it on their own terms. We couldn't have done that without the willingness and support of the early Instagrammers we interviewed and featured. They brought our little app to life in ways that we never thought possible, and acted as role models for what today is a truly global phenomenon.

As a community's original leader, you hold the spotlight. I hope that you'll use it wisely and regularly. Build a culture of reciprocity with your storytelling. Proactively seek stories from exceptional members, then share them widely to inspire others to join the fun. In my experience, this cycle of storytelling won't just move existing and prospective members. It will also bring so much meaning to you and your work. It certainly did for me.

Review Attract new folks

If existing members are helping you grow the community, you'll reach more people, and in a more authentic way, than you ever could alone.

To attract new folks, make sure that you've pinned down the answers to these questions:

1. **What's your story of self, us, and now?**
    Give existing (and prospective!) members the origin story so that they can explain to others *why* your group exists. Make it readily available for all who seek it.

2. **What are the right shareable assets for your community?**
    Make it clear to members that you want their help with recruiting. Then serve up assets that members will be excited to use when telling friends about the community, à la Downtown Girls Basketball and its weekly team pics.

3. **How do you spotlight role models?**
    Collect and share the stories of exceptional members. This will bring the people in your community to life and make them visible to others who are considering joining.

Chapter 5

Cultivate your identity

The little things that members do to express their shared identity will bring them closer together even as the community grows.

In the world of women's professional sports, the Portland Thorns FC are outliers. While most of the teams in the National Women's Soccer League draw an average of 6,000 fans per game, in 2018 the Thorns drew nearly three times as many, averaging over 16,900 fans per game.[28]

What secret sauce makes the Thorns fan base so vibrant?

A 2017 study by Andrew M. Guest and Anne Luijten at the University of Portland revealed an answer. The authors attended Thorns games, conducted 217 surveys with fans, and held extensive interviews with 19 self-identified Thorns supporters. The most-cited reason these people gave for coming to Thorns games was the "atmosphere and supporters culture." Despite the team's two NWSL championships, Thorns players and their victories were less important to fans than was the shared experience of supporting them.[29]

---

28   "Taking Attendance 9/9/2018: NWSL Cracks 6K (Thanks, Addition by Subtraction)" by Kenn Tomasch, kenn.com.

29   "Fan Culture and Motivation in the Context of Successful Women's Professional Team Sports" by Andrew M. Guest and Anne Luijten, *Sport in Society*.

The Rose City Riveters, a group of hardcore fans of the Portland Thorns, are easy to spot in their red gear.

Photo by Corri Goates

A group of hardcore Thorns supporters known as the Rose City Riveters built the foundation of that fan culture.[30] Some of the early Riveters had been female members of the Timbers Army, the infamous fan club that supports Portland's men's soccer team, which shares a stadium with the Thorns. When a women's team came to town, the fans' enthusiasm only intensified. As Riveters steering committee member Jo Thomson, who started as a Timbers supporter, tells us, "I wanted to attend *women's* sports, not just sports. I was 20 times as excited for there to be a women's team as I had been for the Timbers."

These early leaders were the architects of the Thorns' extraordinary fan culture. The Riveters developed chants, selected capos (fans who lead their section of the stands in chants), and distributed lyrics sheets

---

30   "A Blueprint for Women's Sports Success. But Can It Be Copied?" by Caitlin Murray, *The New York Times.*

Riveters in the "North End" section stand, chant, drum, wave flags, raise banners, and blow red smoke in the air.

Photo by Corri Goates

at games. They created elaborate tifos (those ambitious, choreographed visual showings of fan support), and rocked custom scarves. Today, their presence is unmistakable: a crowd clad in red and black outfits fills the "North End" stands at Providence Park during every Thorns game. The Riveters' coordinated chants can be heard blocks away from the stadium.

All of these acts of expression come together to create a bold signal that Thorns fans take women's soccer seriously. Jo explains, "Many people expect women's soccer to be 'soccer light'—to be a notch below the men's games and for fans to treat it like it's a notch below. But that's not what it is in Portland. It's as serious as a heart attack." Jo tells us that she sees the flags, gear, chants, and smoke effects as "an immense labor of love" for the female players and their team.

Rapha Cycling Club (RCC) members around the world host hundreds of rides each week, hitting the road together in official gear. For this RCC ride, 38 members from Taiwan, Singapore, Hong Kong, Malaysia, and other places across Asia cycled together through Yilan County, Taiwan.

Photos by Chelsom Tsai

That sincere passion comes through in everything the Riveters create. Their commitment to crafting creative, thoughtful expressions of a shared identity strengthens the bonds between fans, which keeps people coming back to games. It also draws in new supporters.

If members see their involvement in your community as an important part of who they are, they may want to project their pride to the world. Pride is a captivating energy. So be a steward of the visuals, rituals, and language that your people will use to shape their collective identity.

Equip people with badges to show their pride

One way to cultivate your community's identity is to equip enthusiastic members with *badges*. A badge can be anything visual that enables members to telegraph an affiliation. From personalized gear to custom logos, badges can range from professionally designed to DIY.

Rapha is a sleek, premium cycling clothing company based in London. Worldwide, over 13,500 Rapha superfans pay dues every year to join the formal Rapha Cycling Club (RCC).[31] RCC members go on rides and share free coffees in Rapha stores (called "Clubhouses").

They also rock badass RCC gear. These badges allow members to differentiate themselves from the crowd as a certain kind of cyclist. As Robert Alexander writes in a breakdown of RCC:[32]

> "For those who care about what they look like on the bike (not wanting to be covered in neon yellow logos of some French plumbing supplies company) and see cycling as part of a holistic explanation of their existence then the RCC is absolutely made for them."

---

31   "An Open Road" by Simon Mottram, Rapha, Rapha.cc.

32   "The Rapha Cycling Club—What Is It and Should You Join?" by Robert Alexander, GranFondo.com.

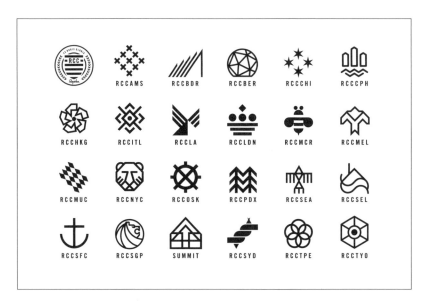

Each Rapha Cycling Club has its own custom seal, inviting members who recognize the familiar emblems to start conversations.

Illustration courtesy of Rapha

Rapha customizes even the smallest aspects of official club gear by city. From bicycle stem caps personalized with member IDs to elaborate welcome packages, the organization shows attention to detail, making badges that are both unique and unified.

These localized details create a "community within a community," Kelton Wright, an RCC Los Angeles member since the group's inception, tells us. "RCC Global is one thing, but when you see the RCC badge of your city on a rider across the globe, it's near mandatory to strike up conversation."

Members wear RCC badges in a display of community solidarity. The badges also allow members to identify and bond with each other. As your own group grows, you may want to consider localizing certain badges to help foster recognition and intimacy between individuals.

Allow new badges to emerge

Badges don't have to be as polished as RCC's. In fact, when you meticulously craft badges *for* members, there can be negative consequences. Supporters may be left with little space for their own voices to be heard.

During the 2016 Democratic primary, Bernie Sanders stoked the enthusiasm of his supporters by letting them participate in shaping his message and visual identity.

Lindsay Ballant, an art director and designer, writes about the difference in badges between supporters of Sanders and those of his opponent Hillary Clinton.[33] In her campaign-branding case study, Lindsay quotes Aled Lewis, an illustrator and a Sanders backer, who commented in a Reddit thread:

> The signs, banners and t-shirts worn and displayed by Bernie supporters [were in] stark contrast to the fresh-out-the-box merchandise that was shipped in by the Hillary campaign. [Hillary supporters] looked like they were in uniforms. The official signs, the gimmicky light-sticks. It looked more like a product launch than a group of supporters.

It would be natural for a community leader to respond to grassroots badges like Bernie's with the urge to "protect the brand," shutting down rogue efforts—but don't! Instead, celebrate the self-expression of your members and encourage them to make their own badges. Whether those badges are physical or digital, the tools for customization are more accessible than ever.

Authentic, shared ownership of the group's identity only fuels a community's fire.

---

33   R/sandersforpresident comment by Aled Lewis, reddit.com. Via "Bernie, Hillary, and the Authenticity Gap: A Case Study in Campaign Branding" by Lindsay Ballant, Medium.

How great is this? No offense, but there's no way that Bernie's team would've come up with it themselves.

Photo by Luke Sharrett/Bloomberg via Getty Images

Codify signature rituals

Bonds between members are fostered through the rituals they practice together, from reciting a mantra to participating in a daily standup meeting. Kursat Ozenc, a designer who researches, writes, and teaches at Stanford's d.school about rituals, notes, "When you practice a ritual that others have practiced before you—or that others are practicing at the same time as you—the actions make you feel connected to them. It takes you out of yourself and makes you part of a larger whole."[34] Established rituals like these have the power to connect new people to members who came before them. That will help your community stick together as it evolves.

---

34   "Introducing Ritual Design: Meaning, Purpose, and Behavior Change" by Kursat Ozenc, Medium: Ritual Design Lab.

94

Tristan Thompson and J.R. Smith share a pregame handshake.

Photo by David Liam Kyle/NBAE via Getty Images

The 2017 Cleveland Cavaliers mastered one of our favorite rituals: the signature handshake. Each of the basketball team's 15 players developed a unique, elaborately choreographed handshake to perform with one another.

Cavs guard Iman Shumpert sparked the tradition. "There's a story behind every handshake," he explained to reporters, noting that each one nods to a player's personal style on the court, their unique sideline cheers, or "something they used to do back home."[35]

Set an intention and develop rituals with your group's key moments in mind. How do we make people feel connected and energized when we get together? Can we help everyone reflect on what we've accomplished at the end of the day?

---

35   "The Story behind the Cavs' Elaborate Pregame Handshakes," YouTube video posted by
        Cleveland Cavaliers on Cleveland.com, youtube.com.

You don't have to meticulously design every ritual. Start by noticing and then codifying the idiosyncrasies that people are already repeating.

Develop a shared language

Another way that people bond over their shared identity is by creating language unique to their community.

Some communities boast an extensive vocabulary in a vernacular that is all their own (e.g., Star Trek fans' grasp of Klingon), but it's not always necessary (or worthwhile) to invent a full language from scratch.

As a start, try agreeing on a name for members. A *demonym* is a word used to describe someone from a certain place. For instance, people from California refer to themselves as Californians. Communities have demonyms, too.

Just as she was breaking into the music scene, Nicki Minaj came up with a demonym for her biggest fans: Barbz, or Barbies. As her career grew, so did the Barbz community. As noted in *The New Yorker*, Minaj has become one of the most celebrated rappers of her generation, and all along she's kept up with her fans—"retweeting them, messaging them, joking around with them, and surveying them about their desires and preferences."[36]

By identifying themselves as Barbz, it's easier for members of the star's fan base to spot each other online—the main place where they gather.

What will your community members call themselves? Here's some inspiration from fan communities that do this really well, in order to get you started.

---

36   "Nicki Minaj's Dark Bargain with Her Fans" by Carrie Battan, *The New Yorker*.

Of course, not every cyclist wants to look like an RCC member. Not every casual Star Trek fan is prepared to learn Klingon. But for some members, badges, rituals, and language are compelling ways to communicate their community-affiliated identity. And when combined with your push to attract new folks, these signature expressions of identity will help the people who jibe with the culture of your community stick together, forming stronger bonds between members. Those bonds lay the groundwork for even more ambitious ways of working together down the line.

Fans of . . .	Are known as . . .
Arsenal FC (Football Club)	Gooners
Beyoncé	Beyhive
BTS	A.R.M.Y. (아미) *(Adorable Representative MC for Youth)*
Female IN	FINsters
Grateful Dead	Deadheads
Green Bay Packers	Cheeseheads
Instant Pot	Potheads
Mariah Carey	Lambs
Marie Kondo	Konverts
My Little Pony	Bronies
Renaissance faires	Rennies
The Beatles	Beatlemaniacs
Urbanist and transit-related content	NUMTOTs
The X-Files	X-Philes
YouTubers John and Hank Green (Vlogbrothers)	Nerdfighters
YouTuber Lilly Singh	Team Super
YouTuber Ryan Higa	Lamps

Review Cultivate your identity

Passionate community members will likely want to project their community identity to the world. These signature expressions encourage stronger bonds between members. To cultivate them, answer:

1. **What *badges* are we promoting?**
    The badges that members use to telegraph their affiliation with your community will vary. While Rapha Cycling Club badges are meticulously designed by the company for its riders, most Bernie Sanders supporters rocked unofficial DIY gear.

2. **What *rituals* are we elevating?**
    Repeat actions, like the Cleveland Cavaliers' handshake ritual, give groups distinct shape. Develop rituals with your group's key moments in mind.

3. **What *language* does our community use?**
    People share identity through words, too. Nicki Minaj's superfans use their community demonym, Barbz, to identify themselves, making it easy for members to spot one another online.

Chapter 6

Pay attention to who keeps showing up

Jennifer Sampson, CEO of United Way of Metropolitan Dallas, once said, "A community is a living organism. It's either declining or improving; there's no steady-state in a community."[37]

As your community expands, how do you know if your work as a leader continues to resonate with your group's purpose?

Don't rely on your instincts. By tracking certain metrics, collecting the right information, and persistently asking questions, you can more accurately understand if your growing community is sticking together. The best place to start is by paying attention to who keeps showing up.

The metric that matters

Tech companies obsess over *user retention*—a metric that captures whether, and how consistently, users return to an experience over time. When you're trying to grow a technology product, retention is the one metric that matters, because a product is only viable if people like it enough to use it again. One-time users can't support a business on their own.

---

37   "7 Things You Have to Do to Build a Powerful Community" by Kevin Daum, *Inc.*

How to keep track of your community

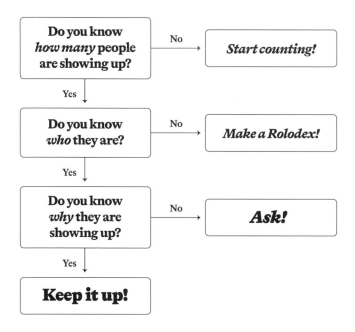

Similarly, a community can only grow sustainably if newcomers find value in their first interactions, then return. If you find that your members aren't consistently participating in or contributing to the group—they're showing up to only one event or sending just one message—you have a leaky bucket. Your community hasn't established the foundation it needs to proliferate.

You can begin tracking and exploring your community's retention in three steps:

1. **Collect participation data.**
    Prioritize the tracking of member participation in community activities. The more the measured action demonstrates true participation, the better. For example, consistently attending a regular event means more than just registering for one gathering but never showing up; posting a thoughtful story signals more interest than simply logging into a forum.

2. **Gather info about your regular participants.**
    Get to know the people who keep showing up. Build a Rolodex that includes notes, like where members are from and contact info. A spreadsheet is a fine start.

3. **Seek insights on why they participate and what they want more of.**
    Listen, listen, and listen. Numbers are great at explaining *how many*, but you'll need to have conversations in order to ask *why?* and discover the root cause of people's motivations. Keep an open line of communication and consider calling members, emailing questions, setting up interviews, or sending surveys.

As we've laid out, don't stop at collecting participation data. It's not enough to measure your community's retention. You need to dig into *who* keeps showing up and *why*. As design researcher and data specialist Arianna McClain writes, people "sometimes resist working with data because all they can see are soulless numbers. When I look at those same numbers, I see human behaviors, needs and motivations."[38] Only a balanced combination of measurement and listening will give you the understanding you need to keep acting in the best interest of an ever-changing community.

Look for hand-raisers

Use your measurement and listening processes to search for people we call "hand-raisers."

These people are your most passionate community members, the hardcore of the hardcore. They always show up. They consistently invite friends. And most importantly, they're raising their hands—eagerly contributing time and energy toward taking your community to the next level.

Hand-raisers have the potential to become homegrown leaders of your community, your most valuable collaborators. If you develop these

---

38   "What Chicken Nuggets Taught Me About Using Data to Design" by Arianna McClain, Medium: IDEO Design x Data.

Sample questions for community member research

1. Can you tell us your name, where you're from, and a few sentences about yourself?

2. How did you hear about this community?

3. Why did you want to be a part of it?

4. What community activities do you participate in?

5. What do you get out of participating?

6. What do you enjoy most? Why?

7. What's frustrating? Why?

8. Are you interested in participating more in the community? What would you like to do?

9. If you could wave a magic wand and summon any tool or resource for community members like yourself, what would you ask for?

10. What other questions should we have asked? Anything else you'd like to share?

hand-raisers, they'll ensure the growth of your community and its ability to stay vibrant. (Find more on how to vet hand-raisers to take on specific roles in **Chapter 7: Create more leaders.**)

So while you're observing how many of your members participate, discovering who they are, and understanding their motivations, zero in on the individuals who are the most engaged. Who seems to be raising their hand to take on bigger responsibilities?

For instance, if you work with a community of volunteers, ask yourself the following questions:

1. **Is there a cohort of ultra-engaged volunteers?**
   Attendance records might reveal that you have a pod of volunteers who never miss a service opportunity.

2. **What does it mean to be ultra-engaged?**
   Do they volunteer more than twice a month? What days? With whom? Which activities or opportunities do they prefer?

3. **Why are they committed to the cause, and what are their aspirations?**
   When you interview your most engaged and active members, you will learn what motivates and inspires these hand-raisers to volunteer. For example, you may meet a former teacher who loves working with kids, and discover that they would jump at the opportunity to lead their own volunteer days.

As philosopher Simone Weil once said, "Attention is the rarest and purest form of generosity."[39] Pay attention to, acknowledge, and listen to your core group. These are passionate people, who will likely delight in the chance to get more involved. Passing the torch to the folks who are raising their hands is how you'll multiply your efforts as a leader and grow together as a community.

---

39   *First and Last Notebooks* by Simone Weil. Via "Simone Weil on Attention and Grace" by Maria Popova, *Brain Pickings*, brainpickings.org.

What to do after a misstep

Rich insights will certainly help you pinpoint future leaders and make decisions that your community will celebrate. But your listening processes are perhaps even more crucial during challenging times. At some point, you may make a change or decision that is not well-received. Paying close attention to your community helps you monitor sentiment, detect your missteps early, and react appropriately.

Mia Quagliarello joined YouTube as the company's very first community manager in 2006, when their small office was still above a pizza shop in San Mateo. As part of her early work there, she handled communication between the company and its users.

This communication proved crucial when the product team redesigned YouTube's "channels." When the team launched the new design, they hit an unexpected nerve with their passionate users. Mia remembers how YouTube's employees "were totally unprepared for how angry people would be."[40] She says, "Your channel is basically your identity on YouTube. I didn't realize how much people's identities were tied up in these online identities. You messed with that, you messed with their space, you messed with their stuff."

After rolling the release back, Mia and her team retooled their communication with the community. This time, they were proactive. Mia assembled a mix of people from the product and community teams together in one room, ready to respond to YouTube community members on social media and help users with their questions. "Not only did this make our coordination and responses more efficient, but also we felt a collective responsibility to do the right thing by our users," she says.

Mia's instinct to be transparent, listen, and acknowledge key stakeholders mirrors fundamental principles from the field of crisis communication.

---

40   "How the YouTube Community Got Its Start: An Interview with Mia Quagliarello, You-Tube's First Community Manager" by Bailey Richardson, Medium: People & Company.

"These platforms would be nothing without the people. They are the lifeblood of the platform, and the customer is always right," says Mia Quagliarello. "So I've learned that at the very least you need to listen and you need to acknowledge and respond—to make the product better, but also make people feel seen who really care."

Photo by Kai Elmer Sotto

"One of the things that is the death knell for a community manager is to not listen," Mia points out. "Even if it's a simple 'Thanks so much for your feedback,' you have to acknowledge people."

Take inspiration from crisis communication experts when you are seeking to remedy a tense situation:[41]

1. **Take ownership quickly.**

   Only when you own your misstep can you begin to earn back respect. As quickly as you can, acknowledge the negative impact of a decision you made. This will help keep fear and distrust from swelling among your members, and will start the healing process.

---

41   Informed by "7 Crisis Communication Tips Every Organization Should Master" by Lauren Landry, Northeastern.edu.

2. **Be transparent.**

   When your community cries foul, you've likely eroded some of the trust that your people had in you, the leader, or in headquarters. You're now under more scrutiny than normal.

   To reestablish trust, be up-front. Provide correct, thorough information and a clear action plan in order to reduce speculation. The more information you hide, the more you risk losing even more trust, damaging relationships beyond repair.

3. **Go deep with key community members.**

   Take extra time to speak with longtime members and emerging leaders in your community about the crisis or conflict. They can help you communicate clearly and sincerely with other members.

Now that you've responded quickly and with transparency, the final step is to internalize what you've learned from the experience. You hit a nerve with your community, and in doing so unearthed something that you didn't know your people were sensitive about. To avoid another challenging situation, allow the knowledge of this sensitivity to inform future decisions that affect your community, and to guide how you'll communicate those changes.

As you face these growing pains, remember: when members communicate frustrations to you, it's a good sign. It means that your people are paying attention and they're invested in this community, just like you.

Review Pay attention to who keeps showing up

By tracking certain metrics, collecting the right information, and asking questions, you can more accurately monitor your community's pulse.

1. **Do we know if members are returning?**
    It's not a community if the members don't come back. Track retention—who keeps showing up and how they're contributing.

2. **Do we know our most passionate members?**
    Spotting your "hand-raisers" is essential to the community's sustainability and growth. Pinpoint the most engaged members in your data and reach out. Ask:

    > Is there a cohort of ultra-engaged members?

    > What does it mean to be ultra-engaged?

    > Why are they committed to the cause, and what are their aspirations?

3. **Do we have a communication plan if we make a misstep?**
    Listen closely for dissent in your community. After a misstep, be prepared to take ownership of your mistake, communicating transparently with key community members.

Stoke the fire: Hear the full stories

Trying to suss out what your growing community needs next? Visit *gettogetherbook.com/stoke* to hear the nitty-gritty from community leaders about how they made sure that their people stuck together.

Listen to Aria share how Downtown Girls Basketball went from a wild idea to a weekly pickup game with a growing roster, dig into an in-depth case study on Rapha Cycling Club's badges, and more.

Pass
the
torch

Growing together

By now, your community has coalesced. Your membership includes regulars who keep showing up. How do you grow into a resilient community that's prepared to realize its purpose for countless others, for years to come?

As our friend Jerri Chou, from The Feast, a dinner series that promotes meaningful conversation, once told us, "a community isn't a community unless it's organizing itself." Whether you want to expand globally or just sustain the magic of your existing group, you will have to pass the torch. Growing together means taking responsibility as a leader to create more leaders. Empowering others to shape your direction is scary, but it's also what makes communities mighty. Spread out ownership by encouraging hand-raisers to lead in ways big and small, supercharging their efforts, and, last but not least, celebrating their accomplishments.

Chapter 7

Create more leaders

What becomes possible when you distribute leadership?

In 2010, a group of Philadelphia K-12 teachers were discussing how out of touch their school's professional development (PD) was. The ongoing training ignored their needs. At worst, the sessions required educators to watch generic PowerPoint presentations from folks who didn't grasp the actual challenges teachers face. What if they flipped that banal teacher development on its head?

A few weeks later, 100 educators gathered on a Saturday at the first Edcamp "unconference": no PowerPoints, no lectures, just teachers learning from each other. Small group discussions on topics ranging from classroom inclusion to "Tech Tools 101" filled the half-day event.

Hadley Ferguson, one of the original Edcamp organizers and the foundation's current executive director, remembers one attendee saying, "This was the best day of training I've had in 20 years." The experience was so refreshing that many attendees asked to bring Edcamp back to their hometowns. Edcamp's founders seized the opportunity to support these newly minted Edcamp leaders and help them facilitate unconferences on their own.

"When you come to Edcamp, what you're going to see, experience, and feel is the connection with other teachers. What you can expect to see, in a word, is 'magic,'" says Edcamp Newark volunteer Juli-Anne Benjamin.[42] Educators like Juli-Anne volunteer to bring the experience of Edcamp professional development to their own areas.

Photos by Paul Jun

42   "Edcamp: Empowering Educators Worldwide #SpreadEdcamp," YouTube video posted by Edcamp Foundation, youtube.com.

Now more than 2,000 educators have helped put on local Edcamps. They've brought together over 150,000 attendees in all 50 states and in 43 countries.[43] One Edcamper we interviewed had attended over 40 events herself! (You'll meet her later in this chapter.) All of this was made possible because Edcamp's founders sought out and teamed up with thousands of volunteers who raised their hands to spread the magic of Edcamp across the globe.

The secret to growing a community

Growing a community isn't about management. It's about developing leaders. With their help, your community will affect more people *and* sustain itself longer than you could have managed on your own.

In any community, a small set of extra-passionate people will do the majority of the work to push the group forward and expand what's possible. As Sam Droege, a biologist, researcher, and veteran organizer of citizen scientists, remarks in Mary Ellen Hannibal's book *Citizen Scientist*, "the bulk of what gets done is by a small set of fanatics."[44] For Sam, that means people like Jane Whittaker, a volunteer bee surveyor who, as Hannibal writes, "has more or less single-handedly inventoried the native bee population of West Virginia." Your community's long-term reach and impact will be determined by your ability to find and empower the right set of leaders, as Sam has done with Jane and Edcamp has done with its volunteers.

But when you're the original leader, trusting others to take over is often a challenge. We get protective, controlling, even paranoid. We worry about people "not having the same standards" or "misrepresenting the brand."

---

43   "The History of Edcamp," Edcamp Foundation, edcamp.org.

44   *Citizen Scientist: Searching for Heroes and Hope in an Age of Extinction* by Mary Ellen Hannibal.

The community spectrum of control

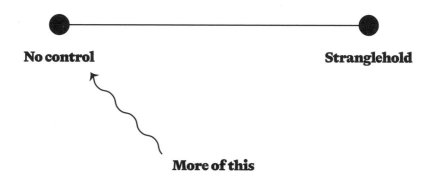

No control   **Stranglehold**

More of this

Don't bend to fears of losing control. As Marshall Ganz says, "Organizers think of themselves as people that develop the leadership of others."[45] You don't have to toil alone. Shift your mindset from *stoking the fire* to *passing the torch*. Your community depends on it.

This shift is imperative for both big and small communities, because cultivating hand-raisers into leaders isn't just a way to expand your reach. It's also the only way that large communities stay relevant over the long term and that small communities ensure their own sustainability. If your community is dependent on a lone leader, it's more at risk of collapse in the face of uncertainty and a changing world.

If you want to maintain your community's magic, bolster its impact, and broaden its reach while honoring the potential of committed community members, you have to empower others.

---

45   "Marshall Ganz: When Did You Start Thinking of Yourself as a Leader?" YouTube video posted by IHI Open School, youtube.com.

What to look for in potential leaders

While Edcamp enables organizers and Sam Droege shepherds super surveyors, community leadership roles can come in all shapes and sizes.

Maybe your business is looking for *ambassadors* to bring the brand to life on the ground. Your nonprofit might be seeking *volunteer coordinators* to catalyze others. Or perhaps your online fan club desperately needs *moderators* to set the tone.

Filling each of these roles requires vetting. So, what do you look for in potential leaders?

Seek genuine and qualified people from your pool of hand-raisers.

Take the brand ambassador role as an example:

1. **Are they *genuine* in their passion for your product and the people who use it?**
    Ideally, they're already avid users (check the data!) or fans of your brand who spend their free time going deep on your product, taking it upon themselves to answer support questions posed by other users.

2. **Are they *qualified* to take on the advocacy responsibilities of an ambassador?**
    Do they communicate passionately and clearly? It's possible that they convey the ins and outs of your product even better than your team can.

For each role in each community, the exact expression of *genuine* and *qualified* will differ. Define what you're filtering for and establish a process that vets for those attributes.

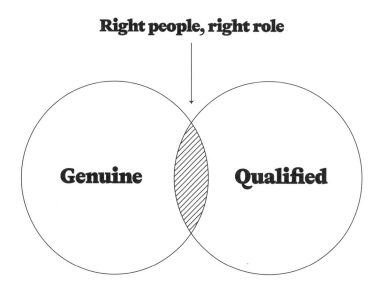

Right people, right role

Genuine   Qualified

What if a leader doesn't work out?

Inevitably, someone who at first seemed like a great fit for a leadership role will end up not working out. Perhaps you misjudged how genuine a leader's motivations were. Or, over time, what your community needed from a leader changed, leaving certain genuine people unqualified for their new responsibilities.

What should you do if you promote the "wrong" leader? Our advice: don't be afraid to say goodbye. Just as an exceptional leader can move a community forward, a bad one can stagnate or, even worse, erode a community's magic.

If a leader breaks the code of conduct that you've established for your community (**Chapter 3: Get people talking**), the decision to part ways might be straightforward. Leaders, even those with minor responsibilities, serve as role models for new members. If a leader isn't setting a great example for others, it may be time for them to move on.

We also recommend defining a process for feedback and reviews with leaders. Consistent check-ins like these carve out space for hard conversations, and also allow for transitions to happen. People—and circumstances—inevitably change. Even the most engaged leaders might relish the opportunity to pass the torch along to someone new. It can be invaluable to set aside regular time to give everyone involved a chance to assess their effectiveness and reflect on their commitment level. Just remember that, as the original leader, you are the one who has the responsibility to prioritize these conversations. Take the initiative.

Finally, what about hand-raisers who crave a leadership role but don't match your "genuine and qualified" criteria? These are some of your most eager, engaged, and loyal community members. To present them with a leadership opportunity only to eventually say "You're not the right fit" sounds like an act of betrayal. Right?

We believe that everyone has a role they can play, and that it's always possible for folks to grow into new roles. Perhaps one of your run crew members isn't ready to lead a run yet, but she can definitely lead the post-workout stretch. Or if a passionate attendee isn't the right fit to co-host, consider letting him take the lead in planning, or asking him to make a short intro onstage. Breaking leadership up into manageable chunks and distributing those nuggets of ownership effectively is part of being a creative, inspiring leader.

What's possible with the right collaborators

It should be clear by now: you can't build a community on your own. One of the great joys of creating more leaders—finding, vetting, and developing them—will be watching some of them far exceed your expectations.

In many of the communities we studied, a core contingent of extra-passionate people made an outsize impact. These exceptional leaders act as catalysts, accelerating a community's ability to fulfill its purpose.

Catalysts are as rare as they are potent. Your job is to seek out these standout leaders, give them the structure and support they need, then let them fly. (There's more on creating a system of support in **Chapter 8: Supercharge your leaders**.)

Here are four catalysts who have inspired us. Through their genuine commitment and exceptional qualifications, they were able to alter the paths of their entire communities for the better.

Bree Nguyen

The superfan who supercharged Mariah Carey's career.

In the 1990s, Mariah Carey was one of the biggest stars in the world, but she had a problem: her fans weren't voting her videos onto MTV's *Total Request Live (TRL)*.

Enter 16-year-old Mariah Carey superfan Bree Nguyen, a kid of the internet and an influential member of the Friends of Mariah online message board.

When the singer announced that she would be doing store signings in three cities in 1999, fans on the message board, in Bree's words, "started freaking out." Bree excitedly announced her plan to attend the LA signing, and when a fellow fan in Brazil asked Bree to deliver a message to Mariah for her, Bree agreed, sharing her email address in a public reply.

By the next day, Bree had received more than 10,000 emails from fans hoping that she'd also take their messages to Mariah. The night before the signing, Bree stayed up until 4:00 a.m. printing fan letters and collecting them in a three-ring binder. She included her own letter at the front, with a heartfelt explanation and her contact info.

At the signing, Bree remembers having "about seven seconds" to pass the binder to Mariah. "I realistically thought that was the end—that the binder was going to be in the dumpster the next day." But three days later, she came home to a voicemail on her machine: "Hi, Bree, it's Mariah.

Mariah Carey. I met you the other day. I'm reading the binder you gave me, and it's the most beautiful thing I've ever received. Please tell the fans thank you."

(Yes, Bree still has a copy of that voicemail.)

Mariah and her team were curious. How did Bree know so many Mariah fans? "I was like, 'The internet,'" Bree says—but Mariah and her team had never heard of the Friends of Mariah fan board. They asked Bree to help get the same fans who wrote letters to vote for Mariah on *TRL*, and offered the superfan a job.

So, at just 16 years old, Bree went on the road with her idol. She taught herself to code and built an online *TRL* voting portal for Mariah's fans, rewarding voters with what she knew they wanted most: access to Mariah (in the form of personal voice messages from the singer, surprises, and gifts). Her work led to Mariah's first ever *TRL* video debut in the top 10,[46] helping the *Rainbow* album go triple platinum.

Today, Bree and Mariah are still friends.

---

46   *Total Request Live: The Ultimate Fan Guide* by Ian Jackman.

Mariah and Bree, still friends 19 years later.

Photos courtesy of Bree Nguyen

"I get a voicemail on my machine: 'Hi, Bree, it's Mariah. Mariah Carey.'"

—Bree Nguyen
  Mariah Carey superfan

Spotlight

Sebastian Betti

The organizing force behind TED's global translation community.

Sebastian Betti of Buenos Aires, Argentina, is the world's most prolific TED Talks translator. Over nine years, he has translated, reviewed, or transcribed nearly 5,000 talks in total.

Sebastian is an avid learner. He taught User Experience Design at Argentina's Universidad Tecnológica Nacional, and is also a computer scientist and ludologist (an expert in the study of games).

While working with universities in the United Kingdom, he was struck by a TED Talk and thought, "Wow, this idea is extraordinary. I would love to share it with my community in Spanish." Sebastian reached out to the TED media team to see if he could help them with a translation. The team told him that they'd received similar requests from people in France, Poland, Italy, and Japan. They suggested that he work with the other translators to establish a more formal program. "That was my first step into the translation community," he says.

When Sebastian began helping the TED team with their early translations, all the volunteer translators worked in silos. "I used to translate every day after work, and I'd deal with so many different topics, from theater to nuclear physics," Sebastian remembers. "I would often have to reach out to experts for help, and I often had technical issues."

To make the process move faster, Sebastian helped coordinate and connect other translators in the TED community to each other and to experts who could fact-check their work. Today, over 33,000 translators have completed more than 140,000 TED Talk translations in 116 languages.[47] "We all rely on each other," Sebastian explains. "At first, it would take me 8-10 hours to complete a translation of a single TED Talk. Now, by collaborating with different teams, I can do 10 to 20 talks a week."

Why stick with TED for so many years? "The translation community lets me cross borders. We address issues from different perspectives in a friendly, pluricentric way," Sebastian says. "And I've been able to meet remarkable people and make lasting friendships in the process."

---

47   "Translate," TED: Ideas Worth Spreading, www.ted.com/translate.

"The translation community lets me cross borders."

—Sebastian Betti
TED translator

Spotlight

Knikole Taylor

The passionate educator who brought Edcamp to southwest Dallas.

Knikole Taylor has known that she wanted to be a teacher since she was in the second grade. "I had an amazing teacher that year—Ms. Carnegie. She made me feel brilliant, special, creative. Like I had something to say, and I needed to be heard," she recalls.

After Knikole earned a degree in finance, her high school principal, who by then was the district's director of human resources, personally reached out and asked her to teach in the same school district she'd attended. "I wanted a job that felt like giving back," she says. "This is my 15th year. I still want to make kids feel the way Ms. Carnegie made me feel about myself."

But in 2013, Knikole fell into a rut with her teaching, and found herself "looking for something to get my spark back." Participating in a Twitter chat for educators, she noticed people talking about Edcamp, a grassroots event where teachers teach teachers on the weekends. "I jumped out of that chat and googled the nearest Edcamp," Knikole remembers.

She drove the four hours from her home in Dallas to an Edcamp in Houston to see what it was all about.

Knikole was hooked: "I was overwhelmed. I learned so much. I couldn't write things down fast enough." She committed to starting an Edcamp

in Dallas, and immediately "started shooting emails out—making connections with people, teachers I knew on Facebook and Twitter," looking for educators to help her organize and attend the first event.

In October, 2015, Knikole hosted her first Edcamp. Local teachers flocked to her school on a Saturday morning. "I mimicked a lot of things I saw at Edcamp Houston and put it together on a smaller scale," Knikole says.

Three years later, Knikole still calls herself an "Edcamp junkie." She's attended more than 40 Edcamps and continues to host her own in Dallas. "If there's an Edcamp within a two-hour radius of my home, I'm probably going," she tells us. Her six-year-old son wants to be a teacher, and has attended Edcamps with her. Her husband tags along sometimes, too.

Knikole's desire to better herself and others as educators stems from her own personal experience with Ms. Carnegie: "Everything I am has come from someone else investing in me. When someone blesses you, in return you should see how you can bless someone else."

134

Knikole Taylor has participated in more than 40 Edcamps.

Photo by Ken Shelton

"Everything I am has come from someone else investing in me."

—Knikole Taylor
  Edcamp SW Dallas organizer

Margret Aldrich

The writer who put a spotlight on Little Free Library's most passionate stewards.

Margret Aldrich is a lifelong lover of reading and language. After pursuing a master's degree in English, she built a career in publishing and journalism, and often devoted her free time to local reading initiatives. So it was no surprise that when Margret saw a Little Free Library, she "just fell in love."[48]

In 2009, Todd Bol put up the very first Little Free Library in his Wisconsin front yard as an ode to his late mother, a devoted reader and educator. His library was a small glass-fronted model of a one-room schoolhouse, which Todd stocked with books that he wanted to give away. The premise was simple: "Take a book, leave a book."

Soon after seeing one herself, Margret decided to erect a Little Free Library in her front yard and register as an official steward with Todd and his nonprofit organization. "As an introvert, I didn't know if I would be a good Little Free Library steward, and then I discovered that it works for anybody," she says. "It's an easy way to connect with the people in your community."

Moved by her experience swapping and sharing books with neighbors, Margret began seeking out other Little Free Library stewards around

---

48   Margret Aldrich on the *Get Together* podcast, episode 5.

the world. She spoke with people like Umayr, a five-year-old boy who put up a library with his father as a way to make new friends when he moved from Canada to Qatar. And Malaz Khojali, a Sudanese woman who is working to bring 100 libraries to her country in an effort to promote literacy.

Margret gathered these stories into a comprehensive book titled *The Little Free Library Book*, which was published in 2015. In addition to spotlighting extraordinary stewards, the book shares the origin story of the organization and offers tips to prospective stewards.

In the course of writing her book, Margret got to know the people behind Little Free Library. "I was head over heels even more, because this is a group of people who is really trying to make a positive difference," she says about the organization. Todd offered Margret a job on the nonprofit's marketing and communications team, and today she continues to spotlight the stewards who have mounted 80,000 Little Free Libraries in 91 countries around the world.

Margret Aldrich (left) poses next to a Little Free Library box with her friend Anitra (right).

Photo by Nathan Kavlie

"When I saw my first Little Free Library, I just fell in love. It's one of those things where you get it right away—I can take one, I can give one."

—Margret Aldrich
Little Free Library steward and storyteller

Review Create more leaders

Growing a community isn't about management. It's about developing leaders. This small set of passionate people will help your community flourish over the long term. To find these leaders, clarify:

1. **What does it mean to be a *qualified* leader in your community?**
   Seek hand-raisers who are experts in a skill you need support for, as Mariah Carey did when she hired internet-savvy whiz kid Bree Nguyen, and as TED did when it asked international teacher and translator Sebastian Betti to coordinate translation efforts. You can create many leadership roles with varying levels of responsibility.

2. **How can you vet for *genuine* leaders?**
   You want leaders who, like Edcamp's Knikole Taylor and Little Free Library's Margret Aldrich, are sincerely motivated by the community's purpose.

3. **What's your feedback process with leaders?**
   Consistent check-ins create a structured, safe space for transitions. If the leader isn't a good fit, don't be afraid to say goodbye.

Notes

_____

_____

_____

_____

_____

_____

_____

_____

_____

_____

_____

_____

_____

_____

_____

_____

_____

_____

Chapter 8

Supercharge your leaders

Now that you've identified and selected leaders, it's time to focus on super-charging their work so that you can accomplish even more together.

Hadley Ferguson, who has helped hundreds of new Edcamp organizers like Knikole Taylor get up and running, tells us that the art of supporting volunteer organizers lies in balancing structure and freedom. "When you challenge people to step up into leadership roles, give just enough structure to make it possible for them to take up that challenge," she advises. With structure, new leaders gain confidence. With freedom, they embrace ownership.

Take inspiration from the Keymaker, a minor character in the sci-fi movie *The Matrix Reloaded*. During the film's climactic chase scene, the Keymaker repeatedly pulls out the right key at the right time to aid in the hero's escape, magically producing keys to open doors, remove locks, and start motorcycles.

In order for leaders to succeed in their respective roles, they need a Keymaker at headquarters backing them up. Strive to provide the support that people need when they need it. Craft ways to help community members save time, grow, and achieve their goals.

A starter map of the journey for an Edcamp organizer who is hosting their first event. Try not to get caught up in the details. Capture the critical activities.

Photo by Kevin Huynh

Map out the leader journey

All right, Keymaker, how do you figure out what support is needed by your community leaders, and when? Your goal is to create a potent system of support instead of a bunch of disparate, semi-helpful resources. Start by mapping out the journey of the person you're trying to help, using good ol' pen and paper.

To get started, assemble a brain trust of your key leaders, and together use Post-its to represent each of the major activities that a certain type of leader is responsible for. The length of the journey you want to optimize is up to you: you can use this approach to map out a leader's day or their first six months in the role.

If this process is new territory for you, we recommend mapping out the leader's main duties over a few months. Get those big responsibilities down on paper and see where you can help.

144

Build out a flowchart of the leader's journey by discussing these questions:

1. What are the first steps that leaders take after raising their hands to accept a leadership role?

2. How are they vetted? Welcomed? Onboarded? Acknowledged?

3. What are the key activities involved in their work? What support do they currently receive?

Identify where leaders need support

With the journey mapped out, talk about which activities add value to this leader's service to the community.

Your support should *supercharge valuable activities* and *minimize or eliminate the others*.[49] In other words, pinpoint activities in which your support can help leaders make a bigger impact or save time.

So, think about three things while reviewing the journey map:

1. Which activities are valuable?

2. Which activities are not as valuable, but are still necessary?

3. Which activities don't help at all?

It's important to revisit your community's purpose during this process. People may have their own sense of what *valuable* means—impact, growth, money—so ground the group's definition in *why* this community comes together in the first place, and prioritize your support against that purpose.

---

49   Informed by Introduction to Lean Six Sigma Methods, lectures delivered by Earll Murman, Hugh McManus, Annalisa Weigel, and Bo Madsen, MIT OpenCourseWare.

How to evaluate activities

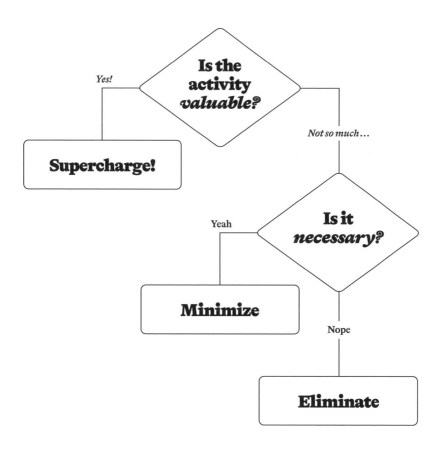

This method of mapping activities is a blend of journey mapping from the field of user experience design and value stream mapping from the lean thinking business methodology.

The answers to your questions should uncover opportunities to support your leaders, as well as generate new ideas about how to help. For example:

1. **Do leaders have major fears about hosting a first meeting?**
   What if there was a formal training?

2. **Do leaders expend hours designing presentations?**
   What if there were templates?

3. **Do leaders waste time searching for files, notes, and other community assets?**
   What if there was one portal with links to everything?

There are many ways to buoy up leaders when they need it. You can host trainings, offer coaching, create templates, assemble a knowledge base, record tutorials, build tools, pre-write emails, develop checklists, collect best practices, start a newsletter, make a FAQ, form partnerships, streamline communications, translate documents, offer funds, line up contacts, lend credibility, buddy people up, send reminders, cut requirements, or even rearrange the order of key activities.

Prioritize figuring out which activities you want to supercharge, minimize, or eliminate, and get creative with how to support the most impactful parts of your leaders' work.

Review Supercharge your leaders

Now that you've selected leaders, it's time to supercharge their work. Your goal is to provide the support that leaders need, when they need it.

1. **What is your leader's journey?**
   Map out your leader's main activities. Ask:

   What are the first steps that leaders take after raising their hands to accept a leadership role?

   How are they vetted? Welcomed? Onboarded? Acknowledged?

   What are the key activities involved in their work? What support do they currently receive?

2. **Where do your leaders most need support?**
   Prioritize opportunities to offer support by deciding:

   Which activities are valuable?

   Which activities are not as valuable, but are still necessary?

   Which activities don't help at all?

3. **How do you provide that support?**
   Figure out which forms of support can add the most value to the work that leaders are doing, as Kevin and his team did for CreativeMornings organizers.

Notes

Before starting People & Company, Kevin took CreativeMornings from four chapters to more than 100. Today, he serves on the board of the Edcamp Foundation and regularly volunteers his time to coach grassroots community leaders. He lives in Brooklyn with his partner Yoko.

Photo by Kai Elmer Sotto

BY KEVIN HUYNH

Embracing process to support your leaders

In college, I spent as much time running a campus events group called SUPERB as I did studying mechanical engineering. I helped 80 student organizers put on more than 100 concerts, film screenings, and comedy shows each year. On a Monday we'd host a sneak preview of the movie *300*. On Wednesday there'd be an open-mic night, and on Friday a standing-room-only concert featuring the hip-hop collective Hieroglyphics.

I remember taking calls between physics and thermodynamics classes to make sure that my event organizers had whatever they needed— last-minute checks, venue permits, an ear to vent to. I loved supporting the staff behind the scenes. That experience flipped a switch in my brain. I witnessed what becomes possible when you empower leaders and back them up when they need it.

After finishing my master's degree, I began my job search, but then I felt a familiar pull. I had this craving to work on a project that got people together. Despite my parents' pleas, I turned down a job at Google and followed my gut to a part-time gig in New York City.

As the son of Vietnamese refugees, I was met with confusion and concern when I chose an unconventional, less stable job. I landed in NYC on a summer night with two big suitcases and a jumble of anxiety, excitement, and determination.

Photo by Tora Chirila for CreativeMornings/Montréal

I showed up as the first paid staff member at CreativeMornings to work with founder Tina Roth Eisenberg, who had pioneered the popular free lecture series in NYC. Events had already spread to three more cities, where morning lectures drew hundreds of creative professionals every month.

I remember logging into our email on my first day. The inbox was full of messages from eager potential organizers hoping to bring a CreativeMornings chapter to their city. Tina gave me the keys— entrusting me to figure out how we'd team up with volunteers, share ownership, and spread CreativeMornings around the world.

One of the first things that I did was map out the ideal journey for a CreativeMornings organizer. I hopped on the phone with current volunteers to understand how they approached their first events. I asked questions like:

Templates, standardized assets, best practices, and other resources ease the journey for CreativeMornings organizers around the world to start their chapters.

Photo by Majid Sadr for CreativeMornings/Tehran

1. What's involved in organizing a lecture?

2. What's the biggest headache?

3. What's the biggest time suck?

4. What was it like planning your first event?

5. How have you changed your planning since?

We used the answers to those questions to plan out the support we'd offer our community leaders throughout their journey. How might we be helpful, from our first contact with them to their 10th event? Kyle Baptista, the current COO and former CreativeMornings/Toronto host, puts it best: "At HQ, you are in *service* of the community."[50]

---

50   Kyle Baptista and Lisa Cifuentes on the *Get Together* podcast, episode 16.

Kevin poses at the first CreativeMornings Summit alongside founder Tina Roth Eisenberg (photobombing on the left) and organizers from Guadalajara, Mexico City, and Singapore.

Photo by Bekka Palmer for CreativeMornings

Over the next three years, my team and I produced a wealth of resources. For instance, we created sample marketing materials. Young chapters used and remixed those assets to establish credibility with potential partners. By the time I left, in 2015, CreativeMornings headquarters supported volunteer organizers in over 100 cities. The number of chapters has almost doubled since.[51]

The approach I took at CreativeMornings wasn't that different from how I solved problems in engineering school. The key is to work systematically: first evaluate, then improve. Campus events, CreativeMornings,

---

51   "Cities," CreativeMornings, creativemornings.com.

and communities that I've worked with since have all affirmed for me that a process-driven mindset reveals just how many opportunities we have to supercharge the work of others.

Apply this approach to your own community. Though the support that leaders need depends on the community they belong to, you can always figure out how to help by breaking down their process. With each step and every activity in their journey, there's an opportunity to make their lives a little easier. Or to save them some time. Or to stir their creativity. Or to make their efforts more effective. Supercharge your leaders and you'll supercharge your impact.

Finally, once you've got foundational resources in place, look to leaders to help each other. Today, CreativeMornings HQ has advanced to the point that HQ team members don't spend much time building resources *for* their community. Instead, they wield their spotlight. They source and reflect back the best practices and resources developed by leaders on the ground.

New leaders breathe life into a community. Embrace process to figure out how to give them the support that they need, every step of the way.

Chapter 9

Celebrate together

Celebrations are festive moments that revitalize a group. Whether they take place under one roof or are synchronized to connect members from separate locations worldwide, celebrations ask everyone tuning in to pause and focus. In these shared moments, we mobilize around where to head next, give our tanks a much-needed refill, and reflect on all that we've accomplished.

For communities, celebrations are not about chasing big crowds or publicity. Instead, they act as motivators—a prime opportunity to move your community forward.

In the book *The Art of Gathering*, Priya Parker, a conflict-resolution mediator, argues that an effective gathering requires a clear purpose. Priya writes:

> When we don't examine the deeper assumptions behind why we gather, we end up skipping too quickly to replicating old, staid formats of gathering. And we forgo the possibility of creating something memorable, even transformative.[52]

---

52 *The Art of Gathering: How We Meet and Why It Matters* by Priya Parker.

Lucasfilm asked Dan Madsen (far left), the head of the Star Wars Fan Club, to spearhead Celebration I. "Lucasfilm really wanted the fan club to own the event," Dan says. "They looked at me and said, 'You have the right amount of professionalism mixed with the right amount of fanaticism.'"[53]

Photo by Rob Deslongchamps, copyright 1999

Nail down the intention of your celebration (which is probably related to your community's overall purpose). Why are you getting everyone together? How does this celebration help your community grow? Parker explains, "Once you have that purpose in mind, you will suddenly find it easier to make all the decisions that a gathering requires." Clarifying the intention of your celebration will bring clarity to all of your logistical decisions, like format, attendees, time, and location.

A celebration to revitalize superfans

The energy of one Star Wars superfan is impressive. Two, awesome. But tens of thousands celebrating in full force could power the Death Star.

---

53   Dan Madsen on the *Get Together* podcast, episode 4.

"I went home with way more friends than when I got there," Brennan Swain says about his experience at the very first Star Wars Celebration.

Photo by Rob Deslongchamps, copyright 1999

That's why, in 1999, Lucasfilm Ltd. decided to reach out to the head of the Official Star Wars Fan Club about organizing the very first Star Wars Celebration. The purpose of the event was to revitalize fans before the release of *Star Wars: Episode I—The Phantom Menace*, the series' first new film in over 16 years. The big event brought 20,000 fans from around the world to Denver, and, not coincidentally, took place just two weeks before *The Phantom Menace* arrived in theaters. Attendees returned home from the Celebration with their passion reignited, itching to queue up for the new Star Wars installment.

Brennan Swain, who has been a Star Wars fan since the night he saw the first film in theaters as a six-year-old, shares what motivated him to show up to Celebration I:

> The movies meant so much to me as a kid. When there was an opportunity to go to this event alongside so many people who had that same love and passion, people who were also eagerly

"We're definitely much more about community—bringing people together and having a good time. The competition is almost the excuse for doing that," says Tim Williams, CEO of the World AeroPress Championship (W.A.C.).

Photo by Glenn Charles Lopez for W.A.C.

awaiting the new movie that would come out soon, I was so excited about that. I couldn't wait for the chance to meet people who were in my online community around the country and the world.

Lucasfilm's first three Star Wars Celebrations coincided with the releases of *Episodes I, II*, and *III*. As Lucasfilm saw attendance grow with each event, the company committed to sustaining the Celebrations.

In April, 2019, 20 years after that first gathering, Lucasfilm hosted its 13th Star Wars Celebration.[54] Organizers estimated that more than 70,000 people flocked to Chicago for the festivities. One of them was Brennan. Why attend another Celebration? He answers, "When *The Force Awakens* came out in 2015, it revitalized my love for Star Wars. I just thought, 'It's time to attend another one of these and see people

54   "Chicago 2019 Star Wars Celebration," Star Wars Celebration, starwarscelebration.com.

Photo by Abi Varney (@abivar) for W.A.C.

I haven't seen in years.'" Even after 13 events and two decades, the Celebration is still doing what it was originally intended to do: rejuvenate the passion of Star Wars' biggest fans.

Choose a format with intention

The Star Wars Celebration had a clear intention: fire up fans in the lead-up to a new film. Lucasfilm's fanfest format realized that intention.

But not every community celebration should be an in-person festival. In fact, if you copy and paste an event that you've seen elsewhere, you likely won't stir *your* people.

Instead, select a format relevant to both your community's identity and its purpose. The right format is crucial to getting your people to come together, and to fulfilling the intention of your celebration.

The founders of the World AeroPress Championship (W.A.C.) opted for a competition format to bring together the planet's geekiest AeroPress baristas.

Why a competition format? When the organizers, internationally renowned baristas Tim Wendelboe and Tim Varney, hosted the first event in 2008, the AeroPress brewing device had only recently been released on the market. The device came with instructions from the inventor, Alan Adler, on how he uses it, but coffee geeks like "the Tims" (who were AeroPress distributors in Norway) thought that they could do better.

Instead of spending months trying to work out how to develop better AeroPress brewing recipes on their own, the Tims decided to crowd-source ideas from other brewers through a small competition in Oslo, which they called the World AeroPress Championship. In the years that followed, fans all around the world asked to lead their own events, and the format began to spread. Each season now sees more than 3,000 competitors go head-to-head in regional showdowns, with one big grand finale to determine a world champion each year.[55]

The W.A.C.'s lighthearted format has fueled its broad appeal. "It's fast-paced, it's super affordable to take part in, and that's really what we found to be a formula that speaks to average people who love coffee," current CEO Tim Williams explains.[56] Unlike more serious barista competitions with lengthy rule books, the W.A.C. has just eight guidelines.

The Tims succeeded in bringing together a loose group of AeroPress fans to test the possibilities of their beloved brewing device. The competition format and simple rules that they decided on fulfill that purpose. Today, the AeroPress community around the world continues to compete in the spirit of exploring what's possible when a simple but powerful tool is placed in curious hands.

---

55   "Our Story (So Far)," World AeroPress Championship, worldaeropresschampionship.com.
56   Tim Williams on the *Get Together* podcast, episode 13.

A young boy negotiates his service fee for a shoeshine in a clip from YouTube's *Life in a Day* film. He and his father were flown out to attend the film's premiere.

Screenshot via YouTube

Celebrations happen online, too

Can an online community celebrate without meeting up in person? Hell yes.

YouTube did just that when it invited members of its international user base to submit footage from their lives on the same day: July 24, 2010.

To bring cohesion to the submissions, users were given a range of prompts, from "What do you love?" and "What do you fear?" to "What's in your pocket?" All in all, 81,000 submissions containing over 4,500 hours of footage from 192 nations were edited into one 90-minute film, which features raw, first-person scenes from real people around the globe, echoing the experience of YouTube itself.[57]

---

57   *Life in a Day: Around the World in 80,000 Clips* by Kevin Macdonald, *The Guardian*.

Posters with song lyrics and large cutouts of musical artists are a few of the many details infused with R&B fandom that make up the special sauce for a 143 celebration.

Photo courtesy of 143 Worldwide

The YouTube community team invited the world to participate in watching the final film, titled *Life in a Day*, just as they'd invited YouTube users to participate in making it. Each contributor was credited as a "co-director" and encouraged to apply to host a screening in their local community. When the film premiered at Sundance, YouTube flew 20 contributors out to attend the screening, and livestreamed the event on YouTube so that thousands more could tune in. Since the 2011 debut of *Life in a Day*, more than 15 million people have watched the film on the site. (You can still watch it there today.)[58]

What motivated YouTube to make such an ambitious feature film *with* its users? Sara Pollack, YouTube's first community manager for film, shares, "The film was made in this amazing period in YouTube's history where we were focused on how we could demonstrate the ways in which

---

58   "Life in a Day," YouTube video posted by Life In A Day, youtube.com.

Photo by Mikey Avila for 143 Worldwide

technology can be both innovative and net positive—how it was driving new ways of storytelling and building community."[59] By selecting an online, collaborative format, YouTube celebrated the unique behavior that its technology enables: creating videos and sharing them without borders. In the process, the site offered YouTubers around the world a chance to join forces with each other, the company, and the movie industry to create something unprecedented.

Don't forget your special sauce

By now, you have a clear intention for your celebration and have selected a format that will realize that intention. Your celebration has direction and structure, a great start.

When you're in the thick of planning, don't forget to honor and incorporate your group's identity. Utilize the idiosyncratic badges, rituals, and language that your community has developed to stick together as you've grown. (Review **Chapter 5: Cultivate your identity**.)

As you plan a celebration for your community, ask yourself:

1. **What are our badges?**
   Rep them together.

2. **What are our rituals?**
   Participate in them as a group.

3. **Got any quirky terminology?**
   Bake your language into the celebration.

Indulge these expressions of your community's identity when you want to spike the energy at your celebration. If you ignore them, then, no matter how refined the purpose or format, your celebration will risk feeling flat. You'll look tone-deaf, or worse: you'll leave your members feeling deflated and disconnected.

---

59   Sara Pollack on the *Get Together* podcast, episode 10.

One group that celebrates with its special sauce front and center is the fan community around the LA-based R&B party called 143. In 2013, three DJs named Partytime, siik, and SOSUPERSAM started 143 to "pay homage to the almighty love song."[60] Today, 143 draws a crowd of thousands, with attendees lining up hours before the doors open.

Though every 143 party feels like a celebration, the group pulls out all the stops for its biggest event, which takes place each year the night before Thanksgiving. It's a party that embodies the community's love for R&B in every detail. From posters customized with Pharrell lyrics to enormous printed cutouts of artists' faces (which are passed around the venue), to surprise performances by Ja Rule and Ashanti, 143 is a celebration deeply infused with the community's appreciation for the genre's music and culture.

Reflect on what you've accomplished

Thriving communities emerge from countless small acts of collaboration. Though they're often hard to notice in the daily toil, these little actions can swell into a serious impact when we undertake them en masse over time.

As a leader, you may be the only person who can clearly see this broader impact. So at your celebrations, take the initiative to reflect on what your community has accomplished together. Cap off your event by bringing to life what your collective acts of devotion have added up to. Whether you've achieved a goal, hit a milestone, or reached an anniversary, you and your people have worked together to push forward your community's purpose. This *why* brought you together in the first place. Your capacity to realize that purpose will continue to bind members together for years to come.

---

60 "1-4-3 MEANS 'I LOVE YOU,'" 143, 143worldwide.com.

Review Celebrate together

Celebrations act as motivators. In these shared moments, we reflect on what we've accomplished, mobilize around where to head next, and give our tanks a much-needed refill.

1. ***Why* are we getting everyone together?**
    Spend time thinking about the intention of your celebration before getting caught up in the logistics. How does this celebration help your community grow? A clear goal (like revitalizing Star Wars fandom) brings clarity to other decisions, like format.

2. **How will we incorporate our community's special sauce?**
    Indulge in expressions of your community's identity. Ask:

    What are your badges? Rep them together.

    What are your rituals? Participate in them as a group.

    Got any quirky terminology? Use it!

3. **What have we accomplished together? How can we reflect on those achievements?**
    As a leader, you may be the only person who can see and bring your community's collective impact to life.

Pass the torch: Hear the full stories

Wondering how to spread ownership and celebrate with your community? Visit ***gettogetherbook.com/pass*** to learn more from leaders who created leaders.

Go deeper with stories about selecting and empowering leaders, including accounts from Tim Williams at the World AeroPress Championship and Margret of Little Free Library. Or hear from Dan about how he managed to pull off such an ambitious Star Wars Celebration for fellow fans.

Notes

In the early 2000s, Kai worked with eBay's community of power sellers. Later, as one of Facebook's early employees, he helped the platform grow to over a billion people. He lives between Singapore and Toronto, and many of the photographs in this book are his.

Photo by Christopher Michel

BY KAI ELMER SOTTO

Remembering our why

I remember the exact moment I went from playing my part as just another eBay employee to feeling like a bona fide member of the eBay community.

In 2002, I joined the fast-growing, six-year-old auction site. The company was no longer just a space to sell your collectible Pez dispensers and Beanie Babies. EBay's pioneering sellers—self-proclaimed "accidental entrepreneurs"—still used the site religiously, but large offline retailers were starting to use eBay as their primary online sales channels. On top of that, the eBay team had scaled quickly.

In response to this expansion, we launched eBay's first in-person celebration, called eBay Live!, in the summer of 2002. The big event was our attempt to rally eBay's diverse stakeholders—employees, small sellers, big corporations, partners—around our shared purpose: the creation of a thriving, accessible online marketplace.

The next year, in a magical moment at eBay Live! in Orlando, we serendipitously introduced a ritual that brought our community closer together.

Kai in the moose mascot costume at eBay Live!, sharing a moment with Gary Briggs, eBay's former CMO of North America.

Photo courtesy of Kai Elmer Sotto

A handful of my colleagues and I had spent three jam-packed days teaching, networking, and listening to sellers of all stripes. A few of us arrived early to the gala dinner we'd planned for the final evening, and we huddled outside waiting for the doors to open. More staff arrived, and we organically formed a tunnel leading to the ballroom entrance.

As sellers arrived and walked down this human tunnel, a few of the eBay staff started giving high fives and hugs to people they recognized. Then we started clapping. The clapping got louder and louder and didn't end. Then PowerSellers started clapping back for us, the employees. The hallways filled with a roar of applause.

More than 15 years later, I still remember clapping for and with those sellers until they passed through the tunnel and were inside the ballroom. I remember cheering on the woman who sold homemade jam and was able to earn enough to surprise her husband by paying off their farm's mortgage. I remember applauding for the Canadian who quadrupled his furniture retail business. I remember high-fiving the developer from Austin, Texas, who grew his sellers app from a startup into a public company. I remember hugging the elderly man who sold collectibles, rolling through the tunnel in his wheelchair.

We were members of the same community, partners in the pursuit of a shared purpose. I wasn't the corporate jerk, sitting in the ivory tower, who doesn't get it. The seller was no longer the squeaky wheel, annoyed about a product change. This moment was physical proof of our gratitude for one another. It was spontaneous and powerful. The clapping tunnel has since become a staple at every eBay Live!, and will remain an essential part of every celebration to come.

What's next for your community?

Now that we've explored the stages of cultivating a community, we're curious: Where are *you* in your community-building journey? Are you just getting started, thinking about how to spark the flame with a group of people? Have you formed your community and are now seeking ways to stoke the fire? Or do you have a thriving group full of potential, and you're wondering how to pass the torch?

Whatever stage you're in, it's crucial to remember that you're working with living, breathing human beings, and, inevitably, some of what results is out of your hands. Over time, you may find that member interest ebbs and flows. That's not unusual. Circumstances change, and growth can make a community that once felt intimate and grassroots feel intimidatingly big and formal (to members, and even to you as an organizer).

Because change is inevitable, don't try to fight it. Instead, build a community that can respond to it.

The goal of this book is to help you foster a supportive, collaborative, and resilient group of human beings. We've showed you how to progressively ask less *from* others and do more *with* them. At each stage, you should have relinquished more of your control and distributed ownership to more and more members.

Our team likes to say the most successful communities are the ones that you couldn't stop from getting together even if you wanted to. Those communities stand to make a truly enduring impact on members, leaders, and even the world.

The alternative to that resilience is an organizational bottleneck. Gavin Pretor-Pinney, the founder of the Cloud Appreciation Society, has found himself in the midst of dealing with just that. He tells us:

> The Cloud Appreciation Society could be so much more if everything didn't have to go through me. Since the beginning, I've done everything. I've designed the website myself and the stuff we sell in our shop. I've written a book, so I've been the one on the TV programs and doing the talks. That's all very well up to a point, and then it just gets to a [place] where we can't go any further. This is the challenge we are facing right now.[61]

Your work isn't done until your members can thrive independent of your time and resources. So ask yourself: Will my community flourish without me? (Will the runners at WRU Crew gather if Hec can't make it? Will members of Female IN find new ways to share stories if Lola takes a break from posting prompts? Will Edcampers keep meeting even without the support of a headquarters?)

If you're not to this point yet, incorporate more listening, invite more participation, and, most crucially, make developing leaders a priority. We know that giving up that control is scary, but we can promise that distributing ownership is both rewarding and necessary. After you light the spark, your community will burn bright and long only once you've truly built it together.

---

61   Gavin Pretor-Pinney on the *Get Together* podcast, episode 2.

"The dream of a peaceful society to me is still the dream of the potluck supper. The society in which all can contribute, and all can find friendship."

—Ursula Franklin
   Physicist, educator, and activist

Appendix

We wrote this book because we want to help more people get their people together. If you're one of those people, or aspire to be, we want to know you. Our aspiration is to bring leaders like you together so that we can help each other build more authentic communities. Without your stories, insights, and energy, we won't get there.

Start by telling us about yourself and the community you're cultivating at:

gettogetherbook.com/hi

If you get in touch with us, we promise to get in touch with you. Together, we can do so much more than we can alone.

Onward!

Checklist How to build a community *with* your people

Where are you in your community-building journey? Use this check-list to pinpoint your next priority or identify a step that you missed along the way.

Spark the flame Getting together

1. **Pinpoint your people**

   ☐ Write down the community's **purpose**: *who* this community brings together and *why* we want to come together.

   ☐ List out your potential early allies (your "**kindling**").

2. **Do something together**

   ☐ Get people together for the first shared activity. Make it **purposeful** and **participatory**.

   ☐ If people are hungry for more, **repeat!** If not, go back to the drawing board.

3. **Get people talking**

   ☐ Create a **space** for members to continue their conversations.

   ☐ **Prompt** conversations so that newbies feel welcome to participate.

   ☐ Establish a code of conduct, moderators, and other **structure** to focus conversations.

Stoke the fire Sticking together

4. **Attract new folks**

   ☐ Make the community's **origin story** available for anyone who seeks it.

   ☐ Equip members to **share** their own stories with the world.

   ☐ **Spotlight** exceptional members to bring the community to life for people who would consider joining.

5. **Cultivate your identity**

   ☐ Help members rep the community's identity with visual **badges**.

   ☐ Elevate signature **rituals** that bond your members.

   ☐ Develop your unique shared **language**.

6. **Pay attention to who keeps showing up**

   ☐ Track member **retention** to make sure that the community remains healthy as it grows.

   ☐ Pay close attention to the most engaged members. (These **hand-raisers** are future leaders!)

   ☐ Prepare to take ownership and communicate transparently with key members if you make a misstep.

Pass the torch Growing together

7. **Create more leaders**

    ☐ Define what it means to be **qualified** for leadership roles.

    ☐ Find ways to vet potential leaders for **genuine** motivations.

    ☐ Carve out roles with varying levels of responsibility so that members can grow into new positions.

    ☐ Initiate a feedback process with leaders.

8. **Supercharge your leaders**

    ☐ Map out the key steps in **leaders' journeys**.

    ☐ Design support that supercharges valuable activities and minimizes/eliminates the not-so-valuable ones.

9. **Celebrate together**

    ☐ Set a clear **intention**. How will this celebration help your community grow?

    ☐ Make a plan to infuse the community's badges, rituals, and language into the celebration.

    ☐ Capture what you've accomplished together and cap off your celebration by reflecting on those achievements.

Thank yous

To our editor, Hannah Davey. Thank you for making this book immensely clearer, more specific, and more valuable to its readers.

To our champion Brianna Wolfson, designers Tyler Thompson and Kevin Wong, Olivia Chernoff, Shaun Young, Patrick Collison, copy editor Susannah Kemple, Courtland Allen and Matt Richman, our first Stripe supporters, and the rest of the team at Stripe Press. Thank you for believing in us and for turning our text into a beautiful artifact. We're proud, and grateful to be Stripe authors.

To our early readers and mentors for their honest and enthusiastic feedback: Anne Libby, Aria Marinelli, Ashlea Sommer, Carly Ayres, Christina Xu, Craig Pearce, Daylon Soh, Edlyn Yuen, Edythe Hughes, Ekaterina Skorobogatova, Emily Lakin, Eric Antonow, Eva Jellison, Fabrice Nadjari, Fiona Brown, Gary Chou, Gregor Hochmuth, Hannah Ray, Isabel Martinez, Jennifer Azlant, Jessica Kausen, Jessica Shambora, Jiwon Moon, Joshua Orr, Kevin Webb, Kurt Yalcin, Laura Brunow Miner, Leslie Jonath, LiJia Gong, Luisa Brimble, Mackey Saturday, Maria Cacenschi, Marysella Castillo, Miraya Berke, Nick Sullivan, Niko Lazaris, Renyung Ho, Ross Drakes, Ru Hill, Ryan Burg, Sachin Monga, Sally Rumble, Sarah Lidgus, Scott Hunzinger, Toon Carpentier, Travis King, and Yoko Sakao Ohama. Thank you to the community at Orbital for chiming in with the input, answers, and encouragement we needed throughout the entire process.

To People & Company's first fans: Sheila Marcelo, Paul Santos, and Eric Manlunas. And to Julie Kim for believing in this idea as a seedling. Without your confidence in us, this book would not exist.

And to the folks who contributed their voices, visuals, and gut checks to this book. You are our heroes. Thank you for letting us get to know you and share your stories:

Ali Leung, Amy Reeder, Andrew M. Guest, Anne Luijten, Arianna McClain, Aria McManus, Bekka Palmer, Bree Nguyen, Brennan Swain, Brittany Cunningham-Scott, Chelsom Tsai, Corri Goates, Dan Madsen, Ebad Ghafoory, Gavin Pretor-Pinney, Gonzalo Esteguy, Greg Jones, Hadley Ferguson, Hector Espinal, Jo Thomson, Juli-Anne Benjamin, Kate Jhaveri, Kelton Wright, Kelvin Gil, Ken Quemuel, Knikole Taylor, Kursat Ozenc, Kyle Baptista, Lauren Gesswein, Lisa Cifuentes, Lola Omolola, Majid Sadr, Margret Aldrich, Marshall Ganz, Mia Quagliarello, Mike (@Veritas), Nobu Adilman, Jerri Chou, Paul Jun, Priya Parker, Rob Deslongchamps, Robert D. Putnam, Robert Wang, Ryan Fitzgibbon, Tina Roth Eisenberg, Sara Pollack, Sebastian Betti, Scott Heiferman, Taylor Larimore, Tim Williams, and Tora Chirila.

184

Featured quotes

"One of the greatest gifts anybody can give is the inspiration to develop courage. If people feel comfortable enough to develop some courage, then they can do anything they really want to do—why, they can devise their own lives."

The **Maya Angelou quote** is from Maya Angelou's foreword for Jean Nidetch's autobiography. (The two were longtime friends!)

Nidetch, Jean. *The Jean Nidetch Story: An Autobiography*. New York: Weight Watchers Publishing Group. 2009.

"Fires can't be made with dead embers, nor can enthusiasm be stirred by spiritless men."

The **"Baldwin" quote** is often attributed to author James Baldwin without a clear citation. According to Quote Investigator, the earliest match that researchers found was a 1942 New York magazine attributing the quote to simply "Baldwin."

"Enthusiasm (Filler item), Quote Page 8." *Elmira Star-Gazette*, May 2, 1942. Quoted in "Fires Can't Be Made with Dead Embers, Nor Can Enthusiasm Be Stirred by Spiritless Men," Quote Investigator. March 21, 2019. **https://quoteinvestigator.com/2019/03/21/embers/#note-22066-1**.

"The dream of a peaceful society to me is still the dream of the potluck supper. The society in which all can contribute, and all can find friendship."

The **Ursula Franklin quote** is from an interview with Ursula on CBC that we found through Austin Kleon.

"Ursula Franklin Interview with *The Current* on CBC Radio (Part 2 of 2)." YouTube video, 9:39. Posted by "UnionStayshyn," July 29, 2010. **https://www.youtube.com/watch?v= 7UJkrZ396VI**. Quoted in Kleon, Austin. Tumblr. "The dream of a peaceful society to me is still the…" October 12, 2016. **http://tumblr.austinkleon.com/post/151719828466**.

Bibliography

1. Putnam, Robert D. *Bowling Alone: The Collapse and Revival of American Community.* New York: Simon & Schuster, 2000.

2. Espinal, Hector. "006: Hector Espinal Started WRU Crew, a Run Club for His Community in Washington Heights." Interview with Bailey Richardson and Kevin Huynh. *Get Together.* Podcast audio. February 22, 2019. https://gettogether.fm/episodes/006-hector-espinal-started-wru-crew-a.

3. Ewalt, David M. "The ESPN of Video Games." *Forbes.* November 13, 2013. https://www.forbes.com/sites/davidewalt/2013/11/13/the-espn-of-video-games/.

4. "The Twitch Holiday Spectacular." Twitch video. December 14, 2018. https://www.twitch.tv/videos/349003971.

5. "Joining the Affiliate Program." Twitch. Accessed March 5, 2019. https://help.twitch.tv/s/article/joining-the-affiliate-program?language=en_US#faq.

6. Nelsen, Chad. "007: Surfrider CEO Chad Nelsen on How Their Chapters Around the World Join Forces to Protect Our Oceans." Interview with Bailey Richardson and Kevin Huynh. *Get Together.* Podcast audio. March 2, 2019. https://gettogether.fm/episodes/007-surfrider-ceo-chad-nelsen-on-how.

7. "Mission." Surfrider Foundation. Accessed February 26, 2019. https://www.surfrider.org/mission.

8. "Monday Series." We Run Uptown. Accessed February 26, 2019. http://werunuptown.com/.

9. Nidetch, Jean. *The Jean Nidetch Story: An Autobiography.* New York: Weight Watchers International, Inc., 2009.

10. Pretor-Pinney, Gavin. "002: How Gavin Pretor-Pinney Grew the Cloud Appreciation Society to 40,000 Members." Interview with Bailey Richardson and Kevin Huynh. *Get Together.* Podcast audio. December 19, 2018. https://gettogether.fm/episodes/002-how-gavin-pretor-pinney-grew-the.

11. "Cloud Appreciation Society Manifesto." Cloud Appreciation Society. Accessed January 16, 2019. https://cloudappreciationsociety.org/manifesto/.

12. Mooallem, Jon. "The Amateur Cloud Society That (Sort Of) Rattled the Scientific Community." *The New York Times Magazine.* May 8, 2016. https://www.nytimes.com/2016/05/08/magazine/the-amateur-cloud-society-that-sort-of-rattled-the-scientific-community.html.

13. Richardson, Bailey. "How Ryan Fitzgibbon Built *Hello Mr.* Hand-in-Hand with Its Community" Medium: People & Company. July 20, 2017. https://research.people-and.com/how-ryan-fitzgibbon-built-hello-mr-hand-in-hand-with-its-community-cb86fcab7e80.

14. Adilman, Nobu. "009: Nobu Adilman Shares the Story of Choir! Choir! Choir!, a Weekly Choir He and Daveed Goldman Started 10 Years Ago." Interview with Bailey Richardson and Kevin Huynh. *Get Together.* Podcast audio. March 19, 2019. https://gettogether.fm/episodes/008-choir-choir-choir.

15. Ortved, John. "Breathing New Life Into Pop Songs with Choir! Choir! Choir!" *The New Yorker.* June 17, 2016. https://www.newyorker.com/culture/culture-desk/breathing-new-life-into-pop-songs-with-choir-choir-choir.

16. Wang, Robert. "015: Instant Pot CEO Robert Wang on how his small pressure cooker company cultivated a rabid community of "Potheads."" Interview with Bailey Richardson and Kevin Huynh. *Get Together*. Podcast audio. June 6, 2019. https://gettogether.fm/episodes/instant-pot-ceo-robert-wang.

17. "Instant Pot Community." Facebook group. Accessed February 27, 2019. https://www.facebook.com/groups/InstantPotCommunity/.

18. Murphy, Bill, Jr. "Here's the Smart Secret Behind the Most Successful Product on Amazon." *Inc.* January 12, 2018. https://www.inc.com/bill-murphy-jr/heres-secret-strategy-that-keeps-instant-pot-at-top-of-amazon-2-words-facebook-cookbooks.html.

19. Omolola, Lola. "003: How Lola Omolola Started Female IN (FIN), a Private Facebook Group with 1.8 Million+ Members." Interview with Bailey Richardson and Kevin Huynh. *Get Together*. Podcast audio. December 19, 2018. https://gettogether.fm/episodes/003-how-lola-omolola-started-female-in.

20. "Female IN (FIN) - Public." Facebook page. Accessed February 27, 2019. https://www.facebook.com/pg/femaleINFIN/about/.

21. "The Bogleheads®." Bogleheads. Accessed September 25, 2018. https://www.bogleheads.org/wiki/The_Bogleheads%C2%AE.

22. "Board rules." Bogleheads.org. Accessed February 27, 2019. https://www.bogleheads.org/forum/rules.

23. "Your Code of Conduct." Open Source Guides. Accessed February 27, 2019. https://opensource.guide/code-of-conduct/.

24. Ganz, Marshall. "Organizing Notes, Spring 2016." Organizing: People, Power, Change, Harvard University. Course handout. Accessed March 1, 2019. https://projects.iq.harvard.edu/files/ganzorganizing/files/organizing_notes_s2016_2.0_mg.docx.

25. McManus, Aria. "Aria McManus Started Downtown Girls Basketball, a Team for Women 'Who Are Specifically Bad at Basketball.'" Interview with Bailey Richardson and Kevin Huynh. *Get Together*. Podcast audio. April 16, 2019. https://gettogether.fm/episodes/aria-mcmanus-dgbb.

26. "All Events." Changemaker Chats. Accessed January 16, 2019. https://changemakerchat.com/events/.

27. "Changemaker Chats Founders Jessica Johnston and Briana Ferrigno 'Don't Just Want to Hear Success Stories.'" MM.LaFleur: The—M—Dash. July 27, 2018. https://mmlafleur.com/mdash/changemaker-chats-founders-interview.

28. Tomasch, Kenn. "Taking Attendance 9/9/2018: NWSL Cracks 6k (Thanks, Addition by Subtraction)." Kenn.com blog. September 9, 2018. http://www.kenn.com/the_blog/?p=9809.

29. Guest, Andrew M. and Anne Luijten. "Fan Culture and Motivation in the Context of Successful Women's Professional Team Sports: A Mixed-Methods Case Study of Portland Thorns Fandom." *Sport in Society*, 21:7 (2018): 1013–1030. https://doi.org/10.1080/17430437.2017.1346620.

30. Murray, Caitlin. "A Blueprint for Women's Sports Success. But Can It Be Copied?" *The New York Times*. October 13, 2017. https://www.nytimes.com/2017/10/13/sports/soccer/portland-thorns-nwsl.html.

31. Mottram, Simon. "An Open Road." Rapha. Accessed February 7, 2019. https://www.rapha.cc/us/en_US/stories/an-open-road.

32. Alexander, Robert. "The Rapha Cycling Club—What Is It and Should You Join." GranFondo.com. April 14, 2015. https://www.granfondo.com/rapha/517742/the-rapha-cycling-club-what-is-it-and-should-you-join.

33. Lewis, Aled. "R/SandersForPresident" comment. Reddit. January 23, 2016. https://www.reddit.com/r/SandersForPresident/comments/42bb7z/caucusing_in_iowa_get_some_bernie_gear_political/cz9b3ql/. Quoted in Ballant, Lindsay. "Bernie, Hillary, and the Authenticity Gap: A Case Study in Campaign Branding." Medium. March 1, 2016. https://medium.com/@lindsayballant/bernie-hillary-and-the-authenticity-gap-a-case-study-in-campaign-branding-ef46845e11cb.

34. Ozenc, Kursat. "Introducing Ritual Design: Meaning, Purpose, and Behavior Change." Medium: Ritual Design Lab. April 2, 2016. https://medium.com/ritual-design/introducing-ritual-design-meaning-purpose-and-behavior-change-44d26d484edf.

35. "The Story Behind the Cavs' Elaborate Pregame Handshakes," YouTube video, 1:38, "Cleveland Cavaliers on Cleveland.com," June 5, 2017. https://www.youtube.com/watch?v=O9w8_dJIpoM.

36. Battan, Carrie. "Nicki Minaj's Dark Bargain with Her Fans." *The New Yorker* via NewYorker.com. August 22, 2018. https://www.newyorker.com/magazine/2018/09/03/nicki-minajs-dark-bargain-with-her-fans.

37. Daum, Kevin. "7 Things You Have to Do to Build a Powerful Community." *Inc.* February 17, 2017. https://www.inc.com/kevin-daum/7-things-you-have-to-do-to-build-a-powerful-community.html.

38. McClain, Arianna. "What Chicken Nuggets Taught Me About Using Data to Design." Medium: IDEO Design x Data. August 17, 2015. https://medium.com/design-x-data/what-chicken-nuggets-taught-me-about-using-data-to-design-b7d44dc7e855.

39. Richardson, Bailey. "How the YouTube Community Got Its Start: An Interview with Mia Quagliarello, YouTube's First Community Manager." Medium: People & Company. June 21, 2017. https://research.people-and.com/mia-quagliarello-was-youtubes-first-community-manager-28872c4a9ae3.

40. Weil, Simone. *First and Last Notebooks*. London: Oxford University Press, 1970. Quoted in Popova, Maria. "Simone Weil on Attention and Grace." *Brain Pickings*. August 19, 2015. https://www.brainpickings.org/2015/08/19/simone-weil-attention-gravity-and-grace/.

41. Landry, Lauren. "7 Crisis Communication Tips Every Organization Should Master." Northeastern.edu. January 9, 2018. https://www.northeastern.edu/graduate/blog/crisis-communication-tips/.

42. "Edcamp: Empowering Educators Worldwide #SpreadEdcamp." YouTube video, 3:40, "Edcamp Foundation," December 2, 2018. https://www.youtube.com/watch?v=rgIqaduELP0.

43. "The History of Edcamp." Edcamp Foundation. Accessed January 16, 2019. https://www.edcamp.org/about-us.

44. Hannibal, Mary Ellen. *Citizen Scientist: Searching for Heroes and Hope in an Age of Extinction*. New York: The Experiment. 2016.

45. "Marshall Ganz: When Did You Start Thinking of Yourself as a Leader?" YouTube video, 3:20, "IHI Open School," March 17, 2011. https://www.youtube.com/watch?v=dkP4V3602IE.

46. Jackman, Ian. *Total Request Live: The Ultimate Fan Guide*. New York: Pocket Books, 2000.

47. "Translate." TED: Ideas Worth Spreading. Accessed January 16, 2019.
https://www.ted.com/participate/translate.

48. Aldrich, Margret. "005: Today, There Are More Than 80,000 Little Free Libraries in 91
Countries. But the Movement Began with Just One Man in Wisconsin." Interview with
Bailey Richardson and Kevin Huynh. *Get Together*. Podcast audio. February 5, 2019.
https://gettogether.fm/episodes/005-today-there-are-more-than-80000.

49. Murman, Earll, Hugh McManus, Annalisa Weigel, and Bo Madsen. "Introduction
to Lean Six Sigma Methods: Ses. 1–3 Lean Thinking Part 1." Lectures, MIT
OpenCourseWare, January, 2012. https://ocw.mit.edu/courses/aeronautics-and-
astronautics/16-660j-introduction-to-lean-six-sigma-methods-january-iap-2012/lecture-
videos/lean-thinking-part-1/.

50. Baptista, Kyle, and Lisa Cifuentes. "CreativeMornings: Lisa Cifuentes and Kyle Baptista."
Interview with Bailey Richardson and Kevin Huynh. *Get Together*. Podcast audio. June
26, 2019. https://gettogether.fm/episodes/creativemornings.

51. "204 Creative Cities." CreativeMornings. Accessed June 10, 2019.
https://creativemornings.com/cities.

52. Parker, Priya. *The Art of Gathering: How We Meet and Why It Matters*. New York:
Riverhead Books, 2018.

53. Madsen, Dan. "004: Lucasfilm Asked a Star Wars Superfan Named Dan Madsen to
Rebuild Their Fan Community. Dan Nailed It." Interview with Bailey Richardson and
Kevin Huynh. *Get Together*. Podcast audio. January 13, 2019. https://gettogether.fm/
episodes/004-lucasfilm-asked-a-star-wars-superfan.

54. "Chicago 2019 Star Wars Celebration." Star Wars Celebration. Accessed February 26,
2019. https://www.starwarscelebration.com/.

55. "Our Story (So Far)" World AeroPress Championship. Accessed May 9, 2019.
https://www.worldaeropresschampionship.com/story.

56. Williams, Tim. "The World AeroPress Championship Brings Together the Planet's Most
Fun-Loving Baristas. CEO Tim Williams Shares the Story Behind the Phenomenon."
Interview with Bailey Richardson and Kevin Huynh. *Get Together*. Podcast audio. May
18, 2019. https://gettogether.fm/episodes/world-aeropress-championship.

57. Macdonald, Kevin. "Life in a Day: Around the World in 80,000 Clips." *The Guardian*.
June 7, 2011. https://www.theguardian.com/film/2011/jun/07/life-in-a-day-macdonald.

58. "Life in a Day." YouTube video, 1:34:56, "Life in a Day," January 21, 2011.
https://www.youtube.com/watch?v=JaFVr_cJJIY&t=2s.

59. Pollack, Sara. "010: At YouTube, Sara Pollack Made 'Life in a Day,' a Film Made by
YouTubers Around the Globe." Interview with Bailey Richardson and Kevin Huynh.
Get Together. Podcast audio. April 1, 2019. https://gettogether.fm/episodes/youtube-
sara-pollack.

60. "1-4-3 MEANS 'I LOVE YOU.'" 143. Accessed September 26, 2018.
https://143worldwide.com/pages/about.

61. Pretor-Pinney, Gavin. "002: How Gavin Pretor-Pinney Grew the Cloud Appreciation
Society to 40,000 Members." Interview with Bailey Richardson and Kevin Huynh.
Get Together. Podcast audio. December 19, 2018. https://gettogether.fm/episodes/002-
how-gavin-pretor-pinney-grew-the.

Stripe
Press